The Splendors Of
TIBET

The Potala Palace.

The Splendors Of TIBET

Text and Photographs by Audrey Topping

Foreword by Seymour Topping

SINO Publishing Company
New York, New York 10151

Copyright © 1980 Audrey R. Topping

Library of Congress Cataloging in Publication Data

Topping, Audrey.

The splendors of Tibet

Includes Index.

1. Tibet--Description and travel. 2. Topping,
Audrey. I. Title.
DS 786.T63   951'.5   80-21989

Designed by Irene Friedman
Map of Tibet (page 8) by John Leinung

Printed in the United States of America

First Edition

To my father, Chester Ronning,
with love and gratitude.

My special thanks go to Kay Lieberman who typed this manuscript and gave me many helpful suggestions. I am also indebted to my editor David Harrop and designer Irene Friedman for their help and encouragement.

Table Of Contents

FOREWORD
Tibet In Transition To The Modern World

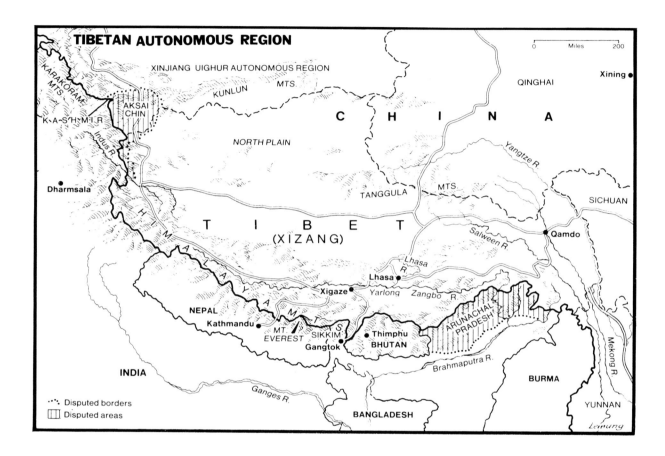

Like a lotus unfolding to the morning sun, Tibet is yielding fresh glimpses of its awesome physical magnificence and stunning Buddhist temple treasures.

For centuries pilgrims, traders and the infrequent foreign adventurer trekked for months by foot, pack mules, horses and yak over precipitous mountain trails to reach Lhasa, holiest city of Buddhism, seat of the Dalai Lama, the spiritual and temporal ruler of Tibet. Even these tortuous paths to the remote "Roof of the World" were barred in 1950 when Chinese Com-

munist troops entered to reassert Peking's historic claim to sovereignty over the country. During the next two decades Tibet was torn by rebellion, turbulent social change and covert foreign intervention. In 1959 the Fourteenth Dalai Lama fled to exile in India as Peking put down an armed revolt of his followers. His domain was formally integrated in 1965 into the political framework of the People's Republic of China as the Tibetan (Xizang) Autonomous Region.

Peking decided in 1976 that internal

8

conditions had been sufficiently stabilized so that a few privileged foreigners could be admitted to Tibet. From the Lanzhou and Chengdu airfields in inland China they were flown to the Lhasa airport, situated 65 miles south of the Tibetan capital in the Yarlung Zangbo River Valley. Braving the moody, often unpredictable, weather over the Tibetan Highlands topped by lofty ice-

teau to Lhasa.

While visas might not be easily forthcoming for years and more adequate hotel facilities are yet to be built, these travel links mean that many sturdy tourists who can tolerate the twelve-thousand-foot altitudes of Lhasa may reasonably look forward to a time when they will behold the wondrous sights described and illustrated

Flying over the Kunlun Mountains to Tibet.

covered peaks, the Chinese established the air connection in 1965.

This air route was one of several projects undertaken to link Tibet to inland China and eventually bring the region more fully into international life. Between 1954 and 1974 the Chinese Communist army, known as the People's Liberation Army (PLA), constructed four motor roads tying the Lhasa road network to four neighboring Chinese provinces. A railroad was under construction in 1980 from Xining in Qinghai Province over the Tibet Pla-

in this book. A few tourist groups visited Lhasa in 1980.

In the fall of 1979 my wife, Audrey Topping, and I visited Tibet on assignment for *The New York Times.* We had sought access for years. Audrey, a freelance photojournalist and author, was permitted to photograph the previously forbidden interiors of the monumental Potala Palace, the great Drepung Monastery and the sacred, bejeweled Buddhist images of the Jokhang Temple, newly reopened by the Chinese authorities for worship. Together we

9

sought in our reportage to penetrate the romantic myths, religious mysticism and the propaganda of both the Chinese Communists and their militant Tibetan refugee foes which had for years obscured Tibet's tragic past and the realities of its present-day condition.

The Tibetan Highlands, homeland of the Tibetan people, embrace the highest and largest plateau in the world (see map). The Highlands are the source of the great rivers — the Yangtze, Mekong, Salween, Brahmaputra and Indus — which water Asia. Tibet comprises three natural divisions. In the Northwest lies the arid, wind-swept great North Plain, jutting up at an average altitude of about three miles. It is dotted with salt lakes and marshes that are separated by mountain ranges and broad valleys. Tibetan nomads tend herds of yaks, sheep and goats in the southern part of the plain. On the northeast, the plateau eases into the high grasslands of Qinghai, while further to the south a series of deep-forested gorges separated by rugged mountain ranges descend into Sichuan Province and Yunnan Province.

The populous cultivated valleys of the south and southeast make up the third and most important topographical division of Tibet. It is here, largely in the Zangpo Valley and its tributary valleys, that the heartland of the present-day Tibetan Autonomous Region lies with Lhasa as its center. This heartland was the focus of the ancient trade routes from India, China and other regions of Central Asia. Today, at altitudes above twelve thousand feet in rarified air and intense sunshine, farmers cultivate barley, millet and winter wheat (introduced by the Chinese) while shepherds take their herds to the grass at the higher altitudes.

Tibet is rimmed by soaring snow-decked mountain ranges whose vastness harmonizes with Buddhist concepts of the infinite and eternal. The North Plain is separated from China's Xinjiang Autonomous Region by the Kunlun Mountains. On the south and west sprawl the Himalayan Mountains with their Karakoram extension on the northwest, dividing Tibet from India, Nepal, Sikkim and Bhutan. Mount Everest, the tallest mountain in the world at 29,028 feet, straddles the Tibet-Nepal border.

Over the centuries the traditional domain of the Tibetan priest-kings was diminished as the British Indian and Chinese empires encroached on areas predominantly populated by Tibetans. Their sway once extended to districts now part of India's Kashmir border area and of Arunachal Pradesh on the northeast frontier as well as border territories of Sikkim, Bhutan and Nepal. Their authority also reached to areas which today are incorporated into the Chinese provinces of Qinghai, Sichuan, Yunnan and Kansu.

The Tibetans are so dispersed — including the 110,000 refugees of the 1959 exodus who live in India, Nepal, Western Europe and North America — that it is difficult to fix their precise demographic locations. According to Peking's 1980 statistics, there were about three million Tibetans living in all of China, including 1.68 million in the Tibetan Autonomous Region itself. Also living in the autonomous region are as many as 120,000 ethnic or Han Chinese and small numbers of Monba, Loba, Hui and Deng minority peoples.

Still other Tibetans who live outside of China are scattered beyond the western and southern fringes of the Tibetan Highlands. En route to Tibet through Northern Pakistan, we made a sidetrip by helicopter into the heart of the Karakoram Mountains and in the remote, exquisite Shiga Valley, we landed at Ashkoli, an isolated Tibetan village. Here, at the furthest outreach of human habitation in the Karakorams, a three-day march from where the nearest jeep track ends, we found people of the Balti tribe, who speak an archaic, classic Tibetan and work as farmers and high altitude porters for mountain climbing expeditions.

The Tibetans are of Mongolian stock, bound together by their Tibetic-Burman language, of which there are several dialects, and their Buddhist faith.

Descendants of the ancient Tibetans still live in Ashkoli, now in Pakistan.

The Chinese claim to sovereignty over Tibet, contested by some Tibetan exiles, has its origins in the thirteenth century when the region came under Mongol influence. In 1578 King Altan Khan, a descendant of Emperor Kublai Khan, bestowed the title of Dalai Lama (Ocean of Wisdom) on Sonam-Gyatso, a Tibetan abbot. Almost a century later, the Fifth Dalai Lama invited Mongol military intervention to crush his Tibetan opponents. When Mongol armies had put down his foes, the Fifth Dalai Lama journeyed to the court of the Ch'ing (Manchu) emperor in Peking where he acknowledged Chinese suzerainty and asked for help in keeping the peace in Tibet.

After the Manchus were ousted and Sun Yat-sen established the Republic of China in 1911, Tibet experienced periods of self-rule. During the Chiang Kai-shek period,

the Chinese maintained a mission in Lhasa but it tended to exercise only nominal authority. In 1949 the Chinese Communists expelled the Chiang Kai-shek armies from the China mainland and the following year marched into Tibet to reassert Peking's historic claim to sovereignty.

Although the government of the Dalai Lama cited evidence of de facto independence, the Tibetans were never able to gain international de jure recognition. The United States, Britain, India and the Soviet Union accepted Chinese suzerainty over Tibet before and after World War II.

In December 1949 the United States secretly rejected an appeal from the government of the Fourteenth Dalai Lama for support in its bid to gain admission to the United Nations as a means of obtaining international recognition of Tibet's indepen-

dence. The State Department instructed the United States Embassy in India to discourage the Tibetans by advising them that such an application would be vetoed by the Soviet and Chinese Nationalist delegations to the Security Council. The State Department also did not wish to antagonize the Chiang Kai-shek government, now installed on Taiwan, which was no less firm than the Communists in asserting Chinese suzerainty over Tibet. In 1950, as the PLA began its march into Tibet, the Dalai Lama's government asked the United Nations for help but thē appeal went unheeded after Britain and India held that the legal claim to independence was not proved.

Advancing on Tibet in October 1950 the PLA met resistance in the eastern district of Qamdo from a Tibetan army commanded by Ngapo Nawang Jigme, a member of the Dalai Lama's cabinet. The Tibetans were defeated and their commander then became an intermediary in peace negotiations between Peking and the Dalai Lama who had fled to India. In April 1951 Ngapo signed a seventeen-point agreement in Peking on "Measures for the Peaceful Liberation of Tibet" and the PLA entered Lhasa peacefully in September.

The agreement provided for "national regional autonomy under the unified leadership of the Central Government." It stated that the central authorities would not alter the existing political system in Tibet and would recognize the established status and powers of the Dalai Lama. Tibetan troops were to be absorbed into the PLA. The agreement also stipulated that "the religious beliefs, customs and habits of the Tibetan People shall be respected." A key article pledged: "On matters relating to various reforms in Tibet, there will be no compulsion . . . the local government of Tibet should carry out reforms on its own accord . . ."

Tibet in 1951 was not the blissful Shangri-la pictured abroad. It was in fact a poor, backward serf society ruled by an aristocracy of monks and noble families

The Indus River flows from Tibet through Pakistan.

headed by the Dalai Lama's theocratic government. Virtually all the grazing and farming land was owned by officials of the government, the monasteries and members of the nobility. The land was tilled and the herds tended by hundreds of thousands of serfs, indentured laborers, many thousands of them bound to the extensive estates owned by the monasteries. The monks preached sacrifice and suffering as preparation for a better incarnate life, and material progress which impinged on tradition was discouraged. While there was respect for life in accordance with the Buddhist ethic, maiming, such as amputation and the gouging out of eyes, and starvation in the dungeons, were sanctioned as punishments for certain crimes. Tibet's population had shrunk from eight million in the eighteenth century to less than half that number as a consequence of inadequate health care and the celibacy of the monks who, in the mid-1950's, numbered an estimated 150,000, one in every four Tibetan males.

When the seventeen-point agreement was signed, the Dalai Lama, then nineteen years old, sent a cable to Chairman Mao Zedong pledging support in the pacification of Tibet and cooperation with China. In July 1952 he left his refuge in the Tunghar monastery near the Indian border and returned to Lhasa. While the Chinese had pledged to respect Tibetan authority and customs, they quickly undertook programs which had the effect of undermining the power of the Tibetan hierarchy. A new class made up largely of poorer Tibetans with a stake in a Communist reform movement began to come into being as schools were established outside of the monasteries and young people were sent to China for higher education. The PLA extended communciations, taught the farmers new methods of cultivation and sent medical teams into the villages. As Chinese influence penetrated Tibetan society fostering this rising sentiment for basic social change, the Dalai Lama sought to regain the initiative by forming a Reforms Committee. The landowning nobles, who controlled the Tibetan bureaucracy, stymied his committee's key proposals for distribution of the land to the serfs and reform of the justice system.

By 1956 Chinese influence had become pervasive and a "preparatory committee," with the Dalai Lama as the figurehead chairman, was set up to prepare Tibet for absorption into the Chinese governmental system. In the same year the Dalai Lama took advantage of a meeting in New Delhi with Premier Nehru, while attending a Buddhist festival, to voice doubts that the Chinese would respect the seventeen-point accord. Premier Zhou En-lai flew to New Delhi to reassure the Dalai Lama and in February 1957, Mao reaffirmed that the agreement would be respected and that the timing of "democratic reforms" would be left to Tibetan leaders. He told a Supreme State Conference in Peking that it had been decided not to proceed with the reforms during the Second Five-Year Plan (1958-62). He also recalled some Chinese officials from Lhasa.

However, these measures came too late. Resentment against the Chinese continued to mount in Tibet among the Tibetan officials, nobles and monks. When the Dalai Lama returned to Tibet, he found the seeds of rebellion firmly sown in the armed monasteries and among the warlike Khamba tribesmen. As early as 1954 the Khambas were conducting raids against the Chinese and this resistance grew into full-scale guerilla warfare by 1957.

The rebels were aided by American and other anti-Communist foreign agents. During 1958 Tibetans were secretly receiving guerilla training from instructors of the Central Intelligence Agency at Camp Hale in the Colorado Rockies, where the terrain and weather conditions approximated those of Tibet. The courses at Camp Hale were conducted until 1961, and graduates were presumably slipped back into Tibet by clandestine means.

Striking militarily at the rebels, the Chinese shelled fortified monasteries and other centers of resistance. The Chinese also asked the Dalai Lama to send his troops against the rebels but he declined. When the fighting spilled into the environs of Lhasa, the Dalai Lama took refuge in the Norbulingka, his summer palace in Jewel Park on the western edge of the city. Torn between the demands of his rebellious retainers and Chinese urgings that he take sanctuary in their military area command, the Dalai Lama decided to flee even as he heard the thud of mortar shells outside the north gate of the palace. On the night of March 17, 1959, accompanied by his family and retainers, he crossed the Kyi River in a yak-skin boat. Horses were waiting for the party and fifteen days later the Dalai Lama crossed the border into India. Scores of thousands of Tibetans followed him into exile.

Within two weeks after the flight of the Dalai Lama, the Chinese garrison had succeeded in ousting hundreds of armed monks from their Lhasa strongholds. The PLA stormed the Chagor Medical Monastery on Iron Hill which overlooked Lhasa and the Potala Palace. Rebels in the Potala and Jokhang Temple ended their resistance after Ngapo, the Dalai Lama's former

13

cabinet minister who had remained in the capital, appealed to them over loudspeakers.

Thousands of PLA reinforcements poured across the Tibetan border, but the struggle went on in some isolated areas for years as the Khamba rebels retreated to bases in India and Nepal. The border raids ceased in 1972 after President Nixon visited China. Thousands were killed in the rebellion and thousands of Tibetans accused of fomenting the conspiracy were imprisoned. We were told in Lhasa that the last of the Tibetan political prisoners were released in 1979. Of the 376 freed at that time, some had been held since 1959, while others had been arrested subsequently as agents sent into Tibet for subversion.

Soon after the fighting in Lhasa ended, the Chinese and their Tibetan supporters proclaimed the "democratic reform" and the government of the Dalai Lama was declared dissolved. Authority was vested in the "preparatory committee" created by the Chinese in 1956. The Dalai Lama was retained as the titular figurehead, while the Panchen Lama, who was the second highest religious dignitary and had remained in Tibet, was named as vice-chairman. For centuries the Chinese had politically exploited power struggles between Dalai Lamas and the Panchen Lamas who resided in a monastery near the city of Xigaze. Now once again confronted with a resisting Dalai Lama, the Chinese used the Panchen Lama to lend legitimacy to their intervention.

As in inland China in the late 1940s, the Communists organized the land-hungry peasants into a mass struggle campaign against the serf owners and all estates of landowners accused of supporting the rebellion were confiscated. The holdings of the others, except for small shares, were purchased by the State and redistributed to the serfs who had been liberated from indentured labor. The monasteries were entered, their property confiscated and the monks dispersed. Some of them became teachers or farmers, while others were enlisted in work gangs or the army. As the "democratic reform" went forward, bloody clashes occurred as monks and other landowners, many of them armed, resisted expropriation by their former serfs.

By 1965 conditions had stabilized sufficiently to allow Peking to go forward with establishment of the Tibetan Autonomous Region within the Chinese political framework. The new regional government was headed by Ngapo. Soon after, Tibet was launched on the collectivist road. Peasants and their land holdings were organized at first into "mutual aid teams" or cooperatives, and then into communes.

In 1966, as in the rest of China, Tibet was suddenly engulfed by the ideological frenzy of the Cultural Revolution. Hundreds, perhaps thousands, were killed or wounded in the fighting in Lhasa and other towns among rival Red Guards made up largely of young Chinese sent to administer Tibet. The guarantees in the seventeen-point agreement of protection for Tibet's religion and culture were scrapped. The Red Guards sacked what remained of the monasteries and also vandalized and closed the Buddhist temples. The Panchen Lama disappeared into prison. When we arrived in Lhasa in 1979, only 10 of the 2,464 monasteries remained intact and the number of monks had declined from 120,000 in 1959 to 2,000.

During the 1960's the Tibetan exiles, headed by the Dalai Lama, who had taken up residence in Dharmsala in northwest India, struggled to win world sympathy for their cause. Some militant exiles caught up in their propaganda war with Peking tended to obscure in the United States and elsewhere the feudal nature of the old Tibet and the extent to which Buddhism there had been tainted by monks who wielded absolute secular power. But in 1963 the Dalai Lama, acting as the leader of a government-in-exile, promulgated what he called a new constitution which he said "takes into consideration the doctrines enunciated by Lord Buddha, the spiritual and temporal heritage of Tibet, and the ideas and ideals of the modern world." The exile government, however, was not able to win formal recognition by the great powers.

United Nation's resolutions, demanding respect for the human rights of the Tibetans, were passed in 1959, 1961 and 1965, but they did not specify violations by China. India, cultivating Peking prior to her border war with China in 1962, did not join in the first two resolutions.

In 1979 the Chinese began to concede openly that they had abused some Tibetan rights and also made errors in managing the economy, particularly during the decade of the Cultural Revolution which ended in 1976 with the death of Mao and the jailing of the "Gang of Four" led by Jiang Jing, Mao's widow. The equivalent of five million dollars was paid to former Tibetan landlords whose property had been seized.

Early in 1979, in keeping with a more tolerant attitude toward religion throughout China, the Jokhang Temple was reopened for worship. The Chinese committed substantial sums to the restoration and maintenance of the Temple, the Potala and the Drepung Monastery. The Panchen Lama reappeared in Peking as a member of the People's Political Consultative Conference, an advisory group of non-political dignitaries. But religion still faced an uncertain future. The state constitution guaranteed "freedom to believe in religion," but also stipulated freedom "to propagate atheism," which was being taught in Tibetan schools. No provision had yet been made for seminary training of youths to replace the aged monks.

Education in general, however, which prior to 1951 could be obtained only in the monasteries or in a few schools for the children of nobles, was rapidly expanded. About 260,000 Tibetans were attending schools and colleges with others being sent to inland China for more advanced education. Most Tibetans over 40 in 1979 were illiterate.

While economic conditions had improved considerably, nevertheless, twenty years after taking full control of Tibet, the Peking government was still struggling with only mixed results to raise the living standards of the Tibetans to the frugal level at which most Chinese lived. Despite substantial investment in roads, factories and farm modernization, progress was slow in expanding food production and accumulating capital to build industry. About 1.2 million of the population was engaged in farming, with 300,000 others in herding and 60,000 in 270 small factories and mines. Tibet is rich in minerals and hydropower potential, but it will take many years before these resources can be substantially developed.

Grain production, which is the principal index of progress and well-being, had more than doubled since 1959. The region became self-sufficient in grain in 1974. But, aside from the rich valleys in which subtopical fruits are raised, many Tibetans were engaged in only bare subsistence farming at altitudes up to 14,000 feet. In the short growing season of about 100 days, their single crops were vulnerable to frost, blizzards, hailstones and sandstorms. Tibetan animal husbandry also lagged behind that of Xinjiang and Inner Mongolia. Efforts had largely failed to crossbreed Tibetan sheep and horses with quality stock brought in from other parts of China. The imported animals, even second-generation crossbreeds, usually cannot endure the high altitudes.

The economy also suffered from a manpower shortage, although the Tibetans have been exempted from the rigorous birth control program in effect in inland China. The birth rate was officially put at 1.8 per cent in 1979 compared with less than 1.2 for the Han Chinese. The Tibetan population increased by about 450,000 between 1959 and 1979.

Throughout Tibet living standards vary widely. Some communes are comparatively well off. Others hover at the poverty line. The contrasts are visible in the market place of the old city quarter of Lhasa, where some peasants shabbily dressed bear the marks of poverty. There are also strong generational contrasts. Tibetans over the age of forty show the physical evidence of malnutrition and lack of health care suffered in their youth. The younger Tibetans appear far healthier in physique. The Chinese have established modern hospitals to supplement traditional Tibetan herbal medicine and sent teams of "barefoot doctors" with six months of training into the villages to provide basic services.

The Han Chinese civilian community in Tibet consisted in 1979 of about 120,000 administrators, technicians, specialists, and some of their family members. The military garrison was estimated by Western observers at 150,000, most of them engaged in construction projects or farming. Unlike other border regions of China, such as Xinjiang, where numerous Han Chinese have settled, there was no indication that such a sinization of Tibet was taking place. Han Chinese have difficulty adjusting physically to the high altitude environment of Tibet. Many leave their families at home for health reasons, and Chinese women stationed in Tibet go home to have their babies. Most officials and specialists are rotated to inland China every three to five years.

Wangdui Zhaba, a Tibetan who headed the Foreign Affairs Bureau, told us that Chinese specialists would be needed for a long time in Tibet, but that some would be replaced by Tibetans as they graduated from colleges and technical schools. He provided these figures on the ethnic composition of the region's administration: on the district level, officials were wholly Tibetan; on the county level, 75 per cent; on the prefectural level, 37 per cent. Tian Bao, a Tibetan who joined the PLA in the thirties, was the chairman of the regional government. Six of his twelve vice-Chairmen were Tibetan.

When we visited Tibet the most powerful official was Ren Rong, a tall Han Chinese in his sixties, who had joined the PLA

as a boy in the thirties, and had been the chief administrator of the region since 1971. We soon heard hints of dissatisfaction with his performance. A working group of the party's Central Committee had come from Peking in August 1979 to investigate conditions.

As we were leaving Tibet in October 1979 we were told casually that a Tibetan delegation, representing the Dalai Lama, was making an unannounced tour of the region. It was headed by his elder brother, Gyalo Thondup. It was the first of several exploratory missions dispatched despite the angry opposition of some Tibetan exiles whom the Dalai Lama described as "radicals." The Chinese had told the Dalai Lama they would welcome his return to Tibet, ostensibly in a religious role but with only nominal political authority.

In April 1980, the forty-six-year-old Dalai Lama told visitors in his retreat at Dharmsala that China's attitude had become "more moderate, more reasonable, more understanding and more realistic," and that he could envision going back to Tibet someday for at least a visit. He spoke of the possibility of a synthesis between Buddhism and the humane aspects of Marxism. But he also cautioned that conditions would have to evolve further since he contended that Tibetans still lived in fear. While he spoke well of Chinese leaders in Peking, he complained about the attitude of the administration in Lhasa.

In May, 1980, while a delegation representing the Tibetan refugee communities of Asia, Western Europe and North America was visiting Tibet, Hu Yaobang, the secretary general of the Chinese Communist Party and Deputy Prime Minister Wan Li arrived for a tour of the region. Hu dismissed Ren Rong as first secretary of the party in Tibet and put in his place Yin Fatang, a Tibetan-speaking Chinese with twenty years of working experience in the region. Denouncing what he called the ultraleftist line of the past, which he said had caused the Tibetan people great suffering, Hu laid down a six-point program to create a more prosperous Tibet.

The program had echoes of the seventeen-point program of 1951 in that it called for the fostering of Tibetan culture, language, education and Buddhist literature. It summoned Tibetan officials to assume the major burdens of leadership and pledged that more than two-thirds of the posts in the regional administration would be held by Tibetans within the next two or three years. Chinese officials were instructed to learn the Tibetan language and to adapt their policies to local conditions and habits. The amount of land allocated to private plots for Tibetan peasants is to be raised to at least 10 per cent and the Tibetans allowed more freedom in selecting agricultural methods. An increase in Peking's financial subsidy was also promised, although it already exceeded any given to the other four autonomous regions and twenty-two provinces. Noting that Tibet constituted one-eighth of the territory of China, the statement declared that the unity of the country could never be assured unless the autonomy rights of the national minorities were respected.

For the Chinese the return of the Dalai Lama would be further evidence that their unity tie with Tibet has been cemented. The problems entailed in achieving such a union were dramatized by the events that erupted in Lhasa in July 1980 near the end of the three-month tour of Tibet by the second delegation of exiles representing the Dalai Lama. When Phuntsog Wangyal, chairman of the exile community in Britain, shouted in a speech to two thousand Tibetans: "May the Dalai Lama's aims and hopes be achieved!," an emotional demonstration broke out. The Lhasa regional government then accused the delegation of having exceeded its brief from the Dalai Lama surreptitiously advocating Tibetan independence, and cut short its tour.

The Dalai Lama laid down in 1979 what he described as three challenges for Peking. The first two have already been met: delegations of Tibetan refugees have been permitted to visit their homeland, and some Tibetans have been allowed to travel abroad. In 1980 the third challenge was yet to be met, that of admitting Tibetan teachers living in the refugee communities to the schools and cultural institutions of Tibet.

In the short span of two decades Tibet has been catapulted into the twentieth century. In the process an intrinsic uniqueness has been lost that set this "Land of Snows" apart from other earthly realms. Tibetan culture, religion and customs, as well as the political institutions and the economy, are undergoing a Communist incarnation which will produce a new society. The precise blend of the socialist forms and the traditional is yet to emerge. Some Tibetans mourn the distinctive heritage that has been lost. Others, particularly the ordinary Tibetan, remembering that in the old serf society there was no political freedom or equality of opportunity, welcome the improvement in living standards. The world will stand watch over the current evolution in Tibet, as never before, for the way to Lhasa is now open.

— *Seymour Topping*

The roof of Jokhang Temple.

1. Journey To Lhasa

View of Lhasa, Abode of the Gods.

The Potala Palace, Home of the Dalai Lamas.

In Tibet all roads lead to the holy city of Lhasa, "The Abode of The Gods," and in Lhasa all eyes turn toward the Potala Palace, the abode on earth of Chenresik, the living incarnation of Buddha, Lord of Compassion, known in the West as the Dalai Lama. The bodies of eight of these God-Kings who once ruled Tibet, have been packed in clay, encrusted with gold leaf and enshrined in individual towers of gold that rise from the depths of the castle-fortress into a burst of gold on the roof of the Potala Palace. On a sunny day the blaze can be seen for miles around.

From the roof of the Potala Palace, the "all-seeing" Dalai Lama could observe the Lhasa valley ringed by the snow-sprinkled Tanggula Hills and watch a glistening blue river named "Waters of Pleasure" running the length of it. Eastward, in the heart of

Lhasa Valley from the Roof of the Potala.

Lhasa, marking the spiritual center of all Tibet, lie the shimmering shrines of the holiest place in the land, the thirteen-hundred-year-old Jokhang Temple. Its original name meant "House of Wisdom," but it is now called "Temple of the Precious One."

In the opposite direction, clinging to a distant hillside, are the tiered white walls of the Drepung Monastery, once a central pillar of the Dalai Lama's theocratic government and home to thousands of crimson-robed lamas. It is known in Tibet as "The Rice Heap."

Today, the Potala Palace, the Jokhang Temple and the Drepung Monastery house the sacred treasures of Lhasa, some of which date back to the Seventh Century, A.D. Now that the mysterious doors of Tibet have finally been opened, selected foreign visitors and devout pilgrims are beginning to enter the once forbidden "Land of Snows." Worshippers with their offerings and prayer wheels now pour into the Jokhang Temple to pray and prostrate themselves before the great golden Buddhas. Others come only to behold the rare and ancient splendors. My husband, Seymour Topping, and I were among the first Western travellers permitted to tour the monumental sites of Lhasa since the abortive armed rebellion against Chinese control of Tibet in 1959. I was accorded special permission by the Tibetan Bureau for the Preservation of Cultural Relics to photograph the interior of these places sacred to the Tibetan people.

The spell of Tibet enveloped us soon after our plane took off from Lanchou, China, as the first streaks of dawn smudged across the horizon like saffron paint over rice paper. Within minutes the world below was lost in white mist. Over the loud speaker a sweet feminine voice said, in stilted English, "Please fasten your seat belts." We looked in vain. There were none. "We are seventeen hundred kilometers from Lhasa. This trip will take two hours and twenty minutes," she continued. Mr. Xie Zhungzhen, a foreign office official

The roof of Jokhang Temple.

Drepung Monastery.

Tibet is isolated by mountain ranges. On the South and Southwest stretch the Himalayas.

from Peking who was accompanying us to Tibet, laughed politely. "She means three hours and twenty minutes," he said. He didn't mention the seat belts.

It was the first trip to Tibet for all three of us, although my husband and I had been dreaming about it for years. For the previous two weeks, we had been touring the adjacent Xinjiang Autonomous Region, and we had just come from the Turfan Valley which, at 470 feet below sea level, is the lowest point in China. Now we were on our way to the highest, Lhasa, which at 12,400 feet above sea level is also the loftiest city in the world.

Suddenly the plane broke through the clouds into a blue dome of sky. Below, the great white tops of the Kunlun Mountains floated like icebergs in a sea of clouds. We were intoxicated by the beauty; yet suddenly it was all gone, sunk into desert,

stretching red and barren, then rippling into sand dunes that rose again into snowy peaks.

The stewardess appeared with cups of steaming jasmine tea. She looked about sixteen. Her thick braids dangled gracefully over her shoulders and a line of controlled curls marched across her forehead. Later we noticed that this was a favorite hair style of the Chinese, or Han, girls in Tibet. As I reached for the tea she intently examined my blond hair and blue eyes before scrutinizing every detail of my clothing. Clearly, Westerners were a rarity in this area. Finally, she smiled reassuringly, deposited some candies on my tray and turned her scrutiny toward my husband. He disarmed her with a wide grin. "Ni hao," (Hello), he said in his halting Chinese. "I'm having a problem getting this seat belt fastened," he continued in Eng-

lish. The stewardess looked puzzled, giggled and handed him some candies.

"She wants you to keep up your sugar level," I said. We had been told that this was necessary at high altitudes.

We flew over range upon range of wondrous, snow-topped mountains. They broke across the Tibetan Highlands in giant waves, frozen forever at the moment of cresting — truly resembling a still photo of an ocean in turmoil. In calmer areas, glimpses of the deep narrow valleys and high plateaus were revealed in hues of ochre, crimson and yellow. The flatlands were studded with sparkling turquoise lakes, and the slopes about them glistened with glacial streams that constantly trickle into the creeks and then tumble into the rivulets — eventually becoming the great rivers of Asia. The Yangtze River, known in Tibet as the Chinsha (Upper Yangtze),

rises from these perpetual snows and begins its plunging, serpentine descent through awesome gorges before it spreads its wings and sweeps across the alluvial plains of Central China. The river finally arrives at Shanghai, one of the largest cities in the world today — built entirely on the silt deposited over the centuries by the great Yangtze.

The Indus River spouts from the melting glaciers on the sacred mountain of Tise, legendary abode of the Hindu God Siva. This vast waterway cleaves its way northwestward, through narrow canyons, picking up speed as it roars through the Karakoram Mountains to water Pakistan. The mighty Yarlung Zangpo River begins its long journey in Tibet cascading from west to east, changing its direction to south and its name to the Brahmaputra River before it flows majestically through India. The

23

Salween, the Mekong and "China's Sorrow," the Yellow River, all spill down from the "Roof of the World" to water the lands of Asia. These rich sources of hydropower have given Tibet a new name: "Reservoir of Asia."

Our spectacular aerial view of the "Land of Snows" impressed on us the remoteness of this mystical land that was left behind while most of the rest of the world had advanced into the twentieth century.

Until 1950 Tibet was a land without wheels. A few Chinese caravans had included carriages, but travel by air, car, wagon or cart was forbidden to the Tibetans. This stemmed from a religious fear of scarring the earth and offending the infinite spirit force — the "Gods of the region," "lords of the ground" and "serpents" believed to dwell in the air as well as the trees, rocks, rivers, mountains and hills of Tibet. These invisible "Mimyin" were credited with both benevolent and

evil powers. If propitiated they could help in time of need, but they could also cause catastrophe if angered. Before the 1950's, when roads for vehicles were constructed, travellers were obliged to walk or ride by yak or pony. High officials and nobles were often carried on the backs of slaves.

Lone travellers and groups of pilgrims would sometimes join caravans for protection against bandits who lived by the thousands in caves carved into the barren hills of the wilder regions, or in nomad tents, from which they set forth to prey on the well-laden caravans. There was, however, a certain honor among these thieves, who were called "Chagba." Being religious men, they would pray before they robbed. They rarely killed and usually left their victims with just enough food and animals to make it to the nearest · shelter. They would even direct them on the quickest way. When the pillage was completed, the brigands would piously share the spoils

On the Northwest border are the Karakorams.

with the nearest monastery to propitiate their sins. Unfortunately, near Lhasa, there were also ruthless killers known as the "Kunma," who were bands of desperate, often maimed criminals who had been driven from the city and survived by robbing pilgrims and other travellers.

Seated in our modern jet, Top and I felt an occasional pang of guilt because our journey to Lhasa was so comfortable. From the window of the plane we caught glimpses of a narrow ribbon of road thrusting steadily on, over the barren plateaus, through the precipitous mountain passes and along the banks of the twisting rivers. In some of the greener valleys it passed little clusters of flat-roofed houses or parts of a crumbling wall, perhaps the ruins of an ancient monastery. It was along this tortuous route that adventurers such as the English explorer Alexandra David-Neel came on foot in 1927, disguised as a Tibetan beggar, determined to witness the pageantry of a Tibetan New Year; and where, in 1846, the Lazarist missionary Abe Huc joined a caravan of 2,000 men, 15,000 yaks, 12,000 camels and 12,000 horses returning from Peking with supplies and chests of treasures for the temples of Lhasa.

For three centuries the holy city of Lhasa had been the lodestone for Asia's devout believers in Tibet's unique form of Buddhism; it was their Mecca, Jerusalem and Lourdes. With their minds oriented toward reincarnation, the fervor of the pilgrims was limitless. Suffering in this life was both retribution for past sins and the means of assurance of a better life in the next incarnation. Throughout the endless journey to Lhasa, the pilgrims would twirl their prayer wheels and mutter the mystic spell of the Lord of Compassion (who was born of a lotus) "Om! ma-ni pad-me Hung!" ("Hail to the jewel in the lotus."). They carried no medicines to cure illness

Buddha of the future.

or weapons to defend themselves.

The more fanatic ones would crawl hundreds of miles on their knees, or measure their length on the ground by prostrating themselves flat, and flat again — like silk worms that inch their way up a mulberry tree to spin cocoons on the highest branches and eventually emerge with wings. This was called "Kyangchhak" or long prostration and considered a high act of holiness which guaranteed rebirth into a better life. Travel by prostration was undertaken most frequently in the fourth month of the year. This month was most auspicious because the fifteenth day of the fourth month of the Tibetan calender was the birthday as well as the day of enlightenment and ascension of the Buddha into Nirvana. Performed at this time, the "Kyangchhak" was believed to bring rewards a thousandfold.

It was not uncommon for pilgrims to

journey all the way from Siberia, Nepal, Kashmir, Bhutan, Sikkim and Mongolia, over 1,000 miles, across the icy, windswept plateaus and snow-covered mountains to fulfill their desire to see the Holy City once before they died. Many perished in the attempt without completing the journey, but this was not considered a tragic or even unhappy event.

Life is but an illusion, the Buddha had said. Reality only exists in the mind. Men observe appearances and disappearances and call them life and death. Thus the arduous journey was considered as important as the goal itself. If death came while making the supreme effort, a better life in the future was assured. The pilgrimages took anywhere from three months to three years. Recalling these epic passages made our short, comfortable trip to Lhasa seem unreal.

Flying over the Tibetan Plateau the stewardess with the curls appeared again to offer us more candies wrapped in edible rice paper. I filled my pockets with the sweet energy which later would serve us well. Soon we were over the Tsangpo Valley and just before landing we circled low over an almost dry, yet green, delta area, then skimmed over some chingko barley and winter wheat fields to the concrete landing strip. On both sides of the runway we could see the indomitable yaks grazing on the sparse pastures. They have become as much a symbol of Tibet as panda bears are a symbol of inland China. These magnificent beasts resemble the American buffalo with long hair and bulging eyes, but they are not as fierce as they appear with their curved horns swooping upwards and their thick fur falling down to their knees like silken robes.

We were met at the airport by Mr. Ke Guangzu, a Han Chinese official from the Foreign Affairs Bureau. We climbed into a Chinese-made car driven by a Tibetan and went north along the Lhasa River, a tributary of the Yarlung Zangpo. One minute we were climbing high along the steep sides and the next we were level with the river. In the back seat was a tank of oxygen. In Peking, before getting permission to travel to Tibet, we had undergone the physical examination required of all foreign visitors to make sure they can tolerate the altitude of Tibet. In the Capital Hospital doctors administered blood tests, cardiographs, liver scans and chest X-rays before we were pronouced fit to journey to the "Roof of the World."

Nevertheless, as we drove over the bumpy, rock-strewn road to Lhasa, Mr. Ke here," he said. "The altitude may cause nausea, leg cramps, chest pains, shortness of breath, dizziness or lightheadedness. But don't worry, in Tibet these phenomena are normal."

At that moment a tire blew and we careened to a stop. I was grateful for the chance to get out, breathe the cyrstal clear air and gaze over the strange, melancholy landscape. Were we really here, in Tibet? I couldn't shake the feeling that it was all an illusion, that I was really inside a glass-

Flat tire on the road to Lhasa.

was full of free advice and warnings about the effects of the lack of oxygen at an altitude of 12,400 feet. Unlike most of the Chinese in Tibet, who consider it a hardship post and rotate every two years, Mr. Ke, who was 52 years old, liked Tibet and had volunteered to stay. After twenty years he had acquired a deep love for the people and his complexion had taken on the ruddy mountain glow typical of Tibetans. "You may experience strange phenomena domed paperweight. The plateau was enclosed in a wide circle of brown foothills, splashed against a turquoise sky and sprinkled with icing sugar snow. The silence, the vast emptiness was startling. The only sound was the crisp rippling of the Lhasa River flowing cleanly beside the road. Some black yaks were grazing in the distance.

My watch said it was ten-thirty in the morning, but the sun was still low over the

27

A dozing cart driver is startled by the rare sight of foreigners.

mountains. As in all of China, Tibet runs on Peking time which puts it two hours ahead of sun-time. It was really eight-thirty in Tibet. This we soon learned did not bother anyone, as the Tibetans run their lives on their own time.

Presently a horse cart loaded with hewn limestone came along. The driver lay atop the pile sound asleep, the reigns dangling loosely from his hand. When he heard the click of my camera he jumped awake and stared at the foreign apparition for a full minute before breaking into a grin. He turned out to be typical of the Tibetans we met, curious but open and friendly with an appealing, trusting innocence. Then, from around the bend came a young woman in a candy-striped apron and green head scarf. She smiled, stopped and posed for a picture as if she did it every day of her life. Following this, a congenial fellow carrying a hoe and pick over his shoulders came along. He seemed delighted to find this diversion and immediately pitched in to help change the tire. Mr. Ke offered him two cigarettes, but he would accept only one.

It seemed that the playful spirits of the hills had arranged our mishap. Along the road to Lhasa we passed piles of stones marking the dwelling places of spirits. Each passing pilgrim would add a stone and respectfully shout "God is victorious," thus paying homage to the invisible forces. This custom had its origin in the ancient primitive religion of Bön which antedated Buddhism as the religion of Tibet.

At the entrance to the bridge crossing to the north side of the river and joining the last stretch of road to Lhasa, we saw a lone guard in the uniform of the People's Liberation Army, shouldering a bayoneted gun. It was the first sign we had seen of the Chinese military presence. Apart from sentries at military headquarters, it was the only time we saw an armed soldier in Tibet although it is estimated by Westerners that there are about 150,000 Peoples Liberation Army, PLA, troops stationed in Tibet, mostly involved in construction projects and land reclamation.

It seemed that the spirits were not finished with us yet. The next tire blew as we were passing a mule caravan campsite. The caravaneers were highly amused at the appearance of our swerving car and gathered around to get a closer look at the strange occupants. The women stood back a bit but the children came running over as if it was all happening for their entertainment. There were about a dozen mule and donkey carts parked along the road, all piled high with chingko barley en route to Lhasa. After some sharp hints from Mr. Ke, the people stopped staring and slowly returned to their morning campfires where tea was being brewed. They began to eat their breakfast from the bowls and spoons which dangled from their belts. It consisted of a mush made of salted chingko barley mixed with thick yak-butter tea, called tsampa. It is one of the staple foods of Tibetans and was also the food of pilgrims as they passed through the country.

Traces of the old pilgrims' route, which mostly runs beside the new road, became more apparent as we got closer to the holy city. The last pass, before the vista of Lhasa unfolded, was protected by a giant bas-relief of a seated Buddha which had been carved into the rock and smudged carefully with a pink powder made from pulverized plants. Its eyes faced towards the Potala Palace.

Our first view of the palace of the Dalai Lamas was staggering. The resplendent, legendary castle of unearthly hues seemed to be levitating in the white sky under a sparkle of golden roof-tops. Then I could see that it was an optical illusion. The crimson palace was actually supported by two white stone wings and a white fortress that soars so naturally from the hill that it was difficult to distinguish the building from the rock. For believers the aura of the Potala must have been immensely magni-

fied by blind faith. I began to understand the spiritual impact this first view had on the pilgrims who had journeyed so far.

Thubten Norbu, a brother of the present fourteenth Dalai Lama, wrote about his first view of the Potala after he had walked and ridden a horse from Kumbum monastery. His journey took three months:

"*. . . rising bold from the lush green valley was the stark red and white fortress, the Potala, its roof of the purest gold seeming to set it afire. . .*

"*It is a sight so beautiful that it struck me with very real shock. I had heard it described so many times, and in such extravagant terms, that I came over the hilltop half feeling that there was nothing new in store for me, that it could scarcely be as inspiring as the endless accounts of it. Yet there it was, and all I could do was rein in my horse and look.*"

In Lhasa the Potala overlooks every-

Rock Sculpture on the road to Lhasa.

The indomitable Yak is native to Tibet.

thing, including the two-storied official guest house where we stayed. This was the only hotel and restaurant in the city and was built in the 1960's. It contains about thirty rooms, and, as in the rest of China, accommodations were not cheap. They cost from U.S. $200.00 to $400.00 per day. This includes three meals, transportation around Lhasa, Tibetan guides, and often a farewell banquet. We had a small but comfortable suite furnished with stuffed sofas and beds you could sink into. Lush Tibetan carpets warmed up the floors and the sitting and bedrooms were separated by plush purple velvet drapes matching those on the windows. Our windows faced south onto a courtyard opening onto the main street. Just outside the open gate there was always a group of curious Tibetans waiting for a look at the visitors. The rooms facing north and east had a spectacular view of the Potala but in the daytime they got steaming hot from the midday sun and were miserably cold after dusk.

Our room boasted an ebony desk with writing necessities, stamps and a short-wave radio but no telephone. A canvas cushion filled with oxygen occupied one chair and another cylinder of it stood ready between the beds in case we experienced any of the "strange phenomena" Mr. Ke had warned us about. I sat on the cushion and put the tube under my nose. After a few deep breaths my lightheadedness subsided.

The roomy bathtub looked most inviting until I felt the glacial waters rushing into it. Then I noticed four enameled thermos bottles full of hot water standing under the sink so I settled for a "lick and a promise." We heard there was hot water in a public bathhouse heated with solar energy and the room attendants assured us that the hotel did have hot water for two hours a day. The only problem was that we could not find out which two hours they were. We only knew that they were not in the morning or evening.

Fuel was obviously a problem in this city above the tree line. Trucks had to bring wood from the southern forests over 250 miles away. The guest house, like the rest of the buildings in Lhasa, went unheated except in the extreme cold but thermal ski pajamas and thick, down comforters kept us warm at night.

After unpacking and putting on our western boots, because this looked like boot country, we accompanied Mr. Xie across the courtyard to another building which housed a large kitchen and dining room with over a dozen large round tables. Mr. Xie left us to sit in lonely splendor behind a wooden screen in the Chinese section while we sat, as the only guests in the foreign section. (We dined with Mr. Xie and his Chinese colleagues on the festive occasions.) Chopsticks, bowls, plates, salted peanuts, beer, tea cups and a selection of cold meats stood on our table. The Chinese cook came out of the kitchen rubbing his hands on his apron and asked Xie to introduce him and to apologize for the humble meal we were about to get. "It is very difficult to get enough vegetables or meat here," the chef said. "I have a terrible time getting the right ingredients but I will do the best I can for you. Please understand."

Without further ado a white smocked

waitress came in with a platter of steaming dumplings stuffed with chopped lamb and onions. This was followed by fried green peppers in soy sauce sprinkled generously with chopped red peppers and sesame seeds. Then came sliced yak meat in tomato sauce, scrambled eggs and sausage, fried sliced potatoes, chopped pork and greens with a black fungus called elephants' ears, steamed rice, roasted sea slugs with button mushrooms and ginger and finally, fried potato pancakes. We ended up with hot sliced cucumbers and egg whites floating in sea weed soup. Everything was extremely tasty. We noticed that the dishes going to Mr. Xie's table were exactly the same as ours.

Afterwards, sated by our "humble" lunch, we were urged by everyone, including the concerned cook and solicitous room attendants, to have a rest. But we could not resist stopping at the hotel gift

An oxygen tank stands between the beds at the Lhasa Guest House.

shop where we bought a Tibetan apron and green silk blouse for me, fancy red felt boots for both of us and a flint bag for Top. Also on display was a variety of dragon-embossed brocades of the type that we later saw draped around the golden Buddhas in the Potala.

The Potala Palace.

Potala rooftops.

2. The Potala: Exploring The Palace Of The Dalai Lamas

The Potala Palace overlooks People's Park.

The legendary palace of the Dalai Lamas of Tibet, the Potala, is actually a giant castle built on top of an ancient fortress which was erected on a rocky peak, called Marpori or Red Hill. The Potala, which in Tibetan means "High Heavenly Realm," is named after a stone cliff on Cape Comorin at the southern tip of India. It was sacred to the Buddha of Compassion, whom the Indians worshiped as Avolokitesvara and the Tibetans believed to be Chenresik, who passed his spirit into the Dalai Lamas.

The Potala is more like an enclosed city than a single building. The outer walls which slope slightly inward enclose a beehive of structures, courtyards and terraces joined together by a series of secret passageways, balconies and winding stairways. The Potala contains two palaces called the White Palace and the Red Palace which together honeycomb a thousand rooms and ten thousand chapels crammed with dozens of thrones for the God-Kings and over 200,000 golden images representing the fantastic pantheon of Lama dieties. The Potala also contains two of the four treasuries in Lhasa, the Trede, reserved for the private use of Dalai Lamas and their Regents, and the Treasury of the Sons of Heaven, for the wealth of the State. The largest portion of the Potala is a vast mausoleum housing the towering golden sepulchers of eight Dalai Lamas and the most sacred area, at the top of the Red Palace, contains the apartments of these consecutive God-Kings and their private monastery "The College of Victorious Heaven."

Below the great structure, in the lower reaches of the fortress are located the vast

The Red Palace houses the private apartments of the God-King.

storerooms once filled with treasure, pilgrim's offerings, volumes of scriptures and many years' supply of yak-butter to fuel the ever-burning votive lamps that stood before each diety. Beside the storage space was a huge, dark printing house where Buddhist scriptures were hand printed. Below all this, carved into the depths of the rock, was the dreaded torture chamber and a dungeon known as the "Cave of Scorpions."

The soaring edifice is a masterpiece of architecture in the traditional Tibetan style. It was the world's tallest skyscraper for over three hundred years but, unlike the Empire State Building, the Eiffel Tower and other buildings that eventually surpassed it in height, it does not have a steel frame. It was built entirely from stone and wood. It towers for thirteen stories, almost a thousand feet, from its rock foundation on the slopes of Red Hill to the top of its golden towers and is even longer than it is high. So much earth was taken from behind Red Hill to mix the mortar for the walls that an artificial lake called Lu Khang was created. Today the lake is known as the Dragon King Pool and a pavilion called the House of the Serpent, built by the Sixth Dalai Lama, stands in its center.

The stone foundation of the Potala was driven deep into the rock and the outer wall, several yards thick, was reinforced by melted copper poured into its middle section to make it earthquake resistant. The upper structure is made of wooden pillars surmounted by Chinese style beams and rafters. The joints of the beams, the brackets and eaves of the roofs of the

Pavilion in the People's Park stands in a lake before the Potala.

main buildings are fitted together without the use of a single nail. The walls and ceilings are spread with a mixture of local earth and lime.

The original Potala, reported to have contained 999 rooms, was built in the early seventh century on the site of an ancient fort by the patron saint of Tibetan Buddhism, King Songtsen Gampo (617-650 A.D.). It was allegedly built for his two foreign wives, a Chinese princess, Wen Cheng, known in Tibet as Gyalza, and a Nepalese princess, Belza. While the King's Tibetan wife was bearing the children, his Chinese and Nepalese wives converted him from the old animistic Bön religion to Mahayana Buddhism. Before that time (400-600 A.D.) the Tibetans were known to be a savage, warlike people whom the Chinese described as "ferocious, barbarian shepherds." Songtsen Gampo unified these warring tribes and at the age of twenty-three made himself King. His armies over-ran Upper Burma and parts of Western China. The young warrior-king was impressed by China's highly developed civilization and threatened to invade the Chinese capital of Chang-an (Sian) unless the

Tang Dynasty Emperor Tai Yang presented him with a bride and dowry. After a period of negotiation, he received the Emperor's adopted daughter, Princess Wen Cheng, who later became a saint of Tibetan Buddhism. Thus began the first relationship in the chain of events that was to link the destinies of Tibet and China until the present time.

Some of the details of this transaction were recorded in Chinese annals of that time: "The Tibetan King erected for her a palace built on Potala Hill with ridge poles and eaves. Moreover he himself put on fine silks and brocades instead of felt and sheepskins, and gradually took to Chinese customs. He sent the children of the chief men to national schools (of China) . . . He asked for silkworm cocoons, for stone crushers, and presses for making wine, and for paper and ink makers. Everything was granted, together with an almanac."

The Tibetan king also sent for Buddhist Scriptures from China and priests from India, where Buddhism was already being overtaken by Hinduism. They brought the

Images of the original builder of the Potala, King Songtsen Gampo (617-650 A.D.) and his two wives.

*Chinese Princess Wen Cheng, wife of
first King, Songtsen Gampo.*

gained power in Tibet, but other aspects of the Bön religion survived. Buddhism in Tibet was never able to completely eliminate those ancestral beliefs and strange rituals which the Bönpoba believed gave them control of supernatural beings and the demonic forces that surrounded them. Instead, Tibetan Buddhism made an effort to absorb these beliefs. Where it could not do this, it garbed the old Bön beliefs in Buddhist robes so the two existed side by side, sometimes merging into one.

A third religious current was the esoteric mysticism of Tantra which includes secret sexual rituals and elements of Hinduism. Tantric Buddhism was introduced into Tibet in the eighth century from India, where it had already been transformed from the pure ethics of early Buddhism. The deities of all three sects: Bön, Tantric Buddhism and Mahayana Buddhism now

Sanskrit sutras, the 'Kangyur' and the 'Tengyur,' that contain the philosophy of Indian Buddhism. King Songtsen Gampo enthusiastically embraced the new religion which became known in Tibet as Vajrayhana, or the Vehicle of the Thunderbolt. The king thus repudiated the old religion called Bön which was based on a kind of Shamanism or devil worship as well as nature worship. The chief practitioners of Bön, called Bönpoba, believed that life was prolonged by extracting the vital force from another living being. They practised exorcism of demons by fire and enhanced the fortunes of the rulers by performing magical rites and ancient rituals.

Important royal funerals required blood sacrifices of many victims, including monkeys, dogs and even humans. These practices were forbidden when Buddhism

A wrathful deity protects the Buddhas in the Potala.

reincarnation, to help all mankind reach paradise. In numerous chapels in the Potala the first king is depicted with a small head of the Buddha of Compassion on top of his turban indicating his incarnation.

During the next centuries Tibet disintegrated once more into warring states and the Potala was severely damaged in the course of tribal warfare and by fires and lightning. By the seventeenth century little was left of the original palace. The Potala that stands today was reconstructed by the Fifth Dalai Lama (1617-1682) known in Tibet as the "Gyalwa Rinpoche" (Dalai Lama) Ngawong Lopsang Gyatso. He began to rebuild the Palace, with the help of the court architect Santi Taso, in 1645. It was an incredible feat nearly comparable to the construction of the Great Wall of China and the pyramids of Egypt.

The image of King Songtsen Gampo stands in the oldest part of the Potala, believed to be his wedding chamber.

stand side by side in the galaxy of Gods in the Potala and temples of Lhasa. The King later became the patron saint of Tibetan Buddhism and was claimed by the Fifth Dalai Lama to be the first reincarnation of Chenresik, the Buddha of Compassion. The Dalai Lamas then assumed that exalted role.

According to Tibetan legend Chenresik was identified with the Compassionate Spirit of the Mountains who bestowed a magic manna on the inhabitants of Tibet and transformed them from apes to men. Then, out of compassion, the Buddha delayed his own passage into the blissful state of Nirvana to stay on earth, through

Statue of thirteenth century reformer Tsongkhapa.

Statue depicting a deity of the ancient Bön religion.

The Fifth Dalai Lama became known as the Great Fifth. He was one of the most masterly figures of the Tibetan chronicles. He was not only the visionary architect of the Potala, but also an outstanding scholar and an adroit but ruthless politician. The Great Fifth led a reform sect called the Galupkas or "yellow hats" which was originally founded in the thirteenth century by a famous reformer Tsongkhapa, whose statues can be seen in many chapels in the Potala.

The Great Fifth gained control of the Middle Region of Tibet, called U, at a critical and chaotic period in Tibetan history. For centuries Tibet had been torn by religious rivalry and constant warfare among the fiefdoms. The followers of the old religion of Bön, who were steeped in occult superstitions, invoked magic spells and the arts of black witchcraft in the struggle to regain supremacy over Buddhism. There was fierce conflict among the monks of the main Buddhist sects who were identified by the color of their hats. The "yellow hats" fought against the Kagupas or "red hats" and the Nyingmapas, "black hats."

The "yellow hats" advocated celibacy and strict discipline. They followed the new translation of the Buddhist sutras, from which demonic influence of Bön had been expunged and the Tantras reappraised, while the other hats, "red and black," adhered to the old translation of the scriptures.

In a desperate attempt to pacify the country and hold power, the Great Fifth made an historic decision that preserved his own rule but acceded to Chinese sovereignty over Tibet. He did this by inviting the intervention of a Mongol Prince. The Mongol was a "yellow hat" Buddhist named Gushri Khan. He was Chief of the powerful Khosot tribe and a great, great grandson of Kubla Khan, the Mongol Emperor of China, who had been converted to Buddhism in the thirteenth century by a Tibetan abbot from the Sakya monastery.

In response, the Mongol armies swept into Tibet, subjugated the Bönpoba and went on to defeat the Great Fifth's prime political enemy, the King of Tsang, Western Tibet, who was allied to the other Buddhist sects. It is interesting in retrospect to note that the Fifth Dalai Lama chose not to annihilate the rival Buddhist sects but left them free to continue in their own way under his rule. He even adopted some aspects of their teaching into the Galupka sect.

The military intervention of the Mongol Prince consolidated the ascendancy of the Galukpas and the rule of the Buddhist theocracy for the next three hundred years. Lopsang Gyatso, now recognized as the "Great Fifth," ascended the throne of a unified Tibet. In return a representative of Prince Gushri Khan remained in Lhasa as military commander with the title of Regent. It was not long, however, before the Dalai Lama replaced the Mongolian with a Tibetan Regent.

To confirm the new peace, the Great Fifth journeyed to Peking for an audience with the Ching Emperor, Shun Zhi, who had just overthrown the Ming Dynasty. The Dalai Lama offered the Emperor his fealty and was confirmed as spiritual and temporal leader of Tibet. The scene was later memorialized in a mural in the Potala.

The Church and State were again merged, as they were previously in the Buddhist theocracy of King Songtsen Gampo in the seventh century. The means of succession to the now celibate high monks became a problem. This was resolved by enlarging on the already accepted theory of reincarnation.

The Fifth Dalai Lama was the fifth Abbot of the "yellow hat" sect, all of whom were regarded as incarnations of the first Abbot. The Fifth now declared that he and his past four predecessors as well as King Songtsen Gampo were reincarnations of Chenresik, Lord of Compassion. They were, he claimed, Buddhisattvas who had delayed entry to Paradise to help others, and further pronounced that all future Dalai Lamas would be of the same reincarnation. He invested himself with the divine right of Kings and, as was often the case in Tibet, "discovered" a hitherto hidden scripture to document his assertion.

To insure support from the conquered kingdom of Tsang, the Dalai Lama shared his divine honors with the abbot of the powerful Tashi Lumpo monastery near Xigaze in western Tibet. The Abbot, who became known as the Tashi or Panchen Lama, was declared to be a reincarnation of "Amitabaha," the Buddha of "Boundless Light." About one thousand other high lamas were eventually declared to be Bodhisattvas of lesser attributes. The Tibetans referred to them as "trulkas" while in the West they were called "Living Buddhas." This theory was accepted by the Tibetans and it soon became the core of Tibetan Buddhism and the source of Lama power.

It was not so easily accepted, however, by the high lamas who were not chosen as divine beings. Those who expressed doubt were cruelly disposed of. The Jesuit Priest Grueber, who in 1656 A.D. visited Lhasa, referred to the Fifth Dalai Lama as "the devilish God-the-father who puts to death such as refuse to adore him."

The Great Fifth further declared that in the future when a Dalai Lama died his spirit would pass out of the corpse into an

The Great Fifth in the later years of his life.

infant boy who had been born at the moment of death. The problem was to find the right child. A group of chosen monks was trained to conduct the search, which took place periodically for the next three centuries.

When the death of the existing Dalai was imminent, the monks began to look for a child bearing the signs of Chenrisik, the Buddha of Compassion. In some cases the dying Dalai Lama would prophesy where his incarnation could be found. Often there were numerous babies born at the same time and the investigation, not always peaceful, lasted for years. The child's body had to conform to the ideal configuration, notably a large head and generous ears, which were considered indicative of wisdom. Marks resembling Buddha's hands, tracing the incumbent form of the Buddha's second pair of arms, had to be perceivable between the shoulder blades.

Oracles and astrologers were consulted and a variety of tests, that included identifying objects belonging to the dead Dalai Lama, would finally establish that the child was the living incarnation of the Dalai Lama. When the child was old enough (from two to six years of age), he was taken from his home by the Regent and high prelates to be trained. The parents of the chosen child, usually of humble origin, were also brought to Lhasa and given noble status. The future spiritual and temporal leader of Tibet was schooled in the Gelukpa doctrine. The Regents exercised full power until the incarnate Buddha reached the age of eighteen.

From the time of the Great Fifth until 1959, the Potala was the center of religious and secular authority. From this castle fortress the God-Kings and their Regents ruled with a mixture of compassion, iron discipline and terror. The Supreme Law was that of the Buddha, as interpreted by the high Lamas. The interpretations, however, varied according to the area, sect, attitude and convenience of the Lamas.

Carrying water up the stairway to the Potala.

The East Portal, 'Door of Happiness.'.

Tibetan Buddhism is often called "Lamaism" in the West because lay Tibetans received all their spiritual guidance from the lama monks. Lama means "teacher" or "superior being" but, although a lama must be a monk, not all monks became lamas. Many of the monks were only humble servants to the higher Lamas, while others lived by begging or dispensing exorcism rites and magical formulae to the superstitious laymen.

The lamas taught that the single purpose of every Tibetan was to come face to face with the supreme truth of existence. While there were different ways of seeking this truth, the main truth in life was suffering. Human suffering was basically caused by the three poisons: "carnal desire," "anger" and "blind passion," (sometimes interpreted as "ignorance.")

Until one could escape desire, one would continue to suffer reincarnation until, by good deeds, meditation and priestly guidance, one was able to achieve the bliss of enlightenment or Nirvana. Bad deeds could cause one to be reborn to one

Over one hundred maintenance workers live in the Potala with their families.

of the three lower stages: an animal, ghost or fiend. But if one obeyed the Law and behaved compassionately towards others, he might be born into a higher station in a future life or even be an incarnate Buddha.

However, according to Buddhist scripture, that was as rare as a one-eyed turtle rising from the ocean every hundred years to poke his head through a floating ox-yoke. Whenever this rare birth did occur, the incarnate Buddhas were 'discovered' and trained to assume the top hierarchical posts in the monasteries or the Potala Palace, under the tutelage of the high Lamas. Besides the Dalai Lama and the lay members of the government, about 154 high prelates ordinarily lived in the Potala in the past. There were also about 200 monks of a lower order, many of them young celibates in training selected from the sons of the aristocracy and government officials.

When we visited the Potala, like the pilgrims and the monks, we entered by climbing the 125 steep stone steps cut into the "Hill of Buddha," which is also called

47

"Red Hill." The steps zigzag across the rock face and split half way up into two directions leading to the East and West Portals. There is no plumbing in the Palace so, when it was occupied by the theocratic government, there was a constant stream of porters carrying water for tea, firewood to feed the braziers in the apartments and yak butter to fuel the prayer lamps that burned before the images. We passed only one porter, a woman carrying water — perhaps for the tea we had later that afternoon in the Dalai Lama's reception room.

The Dalai Lama had a private entrance into the Red Palace which led directly to his apartments. He and the Regent were carried in curtained palanquins that were borne on poles by four men, up the steep narrow road, which curved up the hill at the back of the Palace. They were followed by an entourage of high Lamas who were carried "piggy-back" by servant-bearers. We found it was not so easy to climb the stone steps on foot. I could imagine the strain of an extra burden.

Immediately above the stairway towered the White Palace which contained the offices and the residences of the secular staff members. There was also a school for government officials. The Fifth Dalai Lama

Redecorating the palace.

transferred the government into the White Palace when it was completed in 1653. Behind, and even higher, rises the sacred Red Palace, whose color is symbolic of power and authority. The Red Palace contains the temples, monastic apartments and the monastery of the Dalai Lamas; its construction was begun in 1690.

The East Portal or "Door of Happiness" was hung with dark yak-wool curtains. The inside walls were painted with murals of the four lakapalas or Guardians of the Four Directions. Here we were met by a studious 57-year-old Tibetan named Losang who headed the Lhasa Cultural Relics Commission and was an expert on the Potala. As he conducted us on the tour, he spoke in Tibetan to our Tibetan guide, a young woman with great round eyes, who translated it into Chinese to Mr. Xie our Chinese escort who, in turn, translated it into English for us.

We proceeded through a narrow corridor with blue, red and yellow stripes running along the saffron wall. Bright blue beams supported the yellow ceiling and this intensity of color was enough to make the beholder dizzy. The corridor led into a wide courtyard, the Deyangxar Terrace, where sorcerers' dances, exorcism rituals and theatrical performances were held on holidays and religious festivals. The Dalai Lama and his entourage would watch from the yellow balconies suspended from the south wall of the White Palace.

East of the platform stood the former seminary for senior lamas and on the west side, in a series of yellow enclaves, were the chanting halls and monks' dormitories. In the courtyard we saw some of the one hundred maintenance workers who live in the Palace and have been constantly repairing and repainting the Palace since 1961 when the State Council in Peking placed it on the list of cultural sites to be given special protection. The cost of main-

The funeral stupas of the Dalai Lamas tower three stories to golden canopies on the roof tops. The bodies of eight Dalai Lamas are enshrined in the Potala mausoleum.

tenance, according to Losang, is U.S. $67,-000 per year. There is also a group of Tibetan and Chinese scholars and historians engaged in studying the innumerable objects preserved and stored in the lowest part of the Potala.

On one platform we saw a pile of huge logs that were to be used as replacement pillars. They had been brought by truck on a two-day haul from the southern forests, a distance of 250 miles. The Potala, of course, had been built before the introduction of the wheel into Tibet and its original pillars had been built from logs carried on the backs of men.

Historical records show that over seven thousand laborers, including some craftsmen from China and Nepal, worked for fifty years on the Potala using only primitive tools. Hundreds of others quarried the stone and cut the great logs in the southern pine forests. The stone blocks were brought to Lhasa by donkeys or were lashed with yak-thongs onto the backs of humans, one stone block per person. Un-

The cone-shaped top is made of pure gold.

The base of the tomb of the Fifth Dalai Lama.

50

The East main hall was used for coronations.

Image of the Thirteenth Dalai Lama who died in 1933.

told thousands, including women and children, perished, secure in the belief that they were serving the Lord of Compassion and would therefore be rewarded in the next life. Over half of the workers were serfs who brought their own food and worked without pay. Even so, the cost of the Red Palace alone amounted to 2,134,-136 taels or about four million ounces of silver, a vast figure in those days and simply astronomical for Tibet.

These devout serfs labored ignorant of the fact that their "Living God" was dead. The Great Fifth died in 1682, eight years before the building of the Red Palace was even started. The departure of the Fifth Dalai Lama to the "Heavenly Field" was cleverly concealed for ten years by his Chief Minister, Sanggye Gyatso, who had replaced the Mongol as Regent in 1679. The Regent knew that if the death had become known, the work on the Potala

51

One of hundreds of doors leading to the 999 inner chambers.

PHOTO RIGHT: Buddha of the Past.

The Potala houses a myriad of golden Buddhas.

Darje-Shakpa, with a third eye, is one of four fierce gatekeepers.

Altar in the chapel of Avalokites Wara.　　　　　　　*PHOTO RIGHT: King Songtsen Gampo.*

would certainly have stopped. Instead Sanggye Gyatso, who was rumored to be the son of the Great Fifth, although most historians claim he was only a "spiritual son," assumed supreme power and continued to supervise the construction, allowing the people to believe that the Dalai Lama was living in seclusion, meditating — an explanation that was accepted without question.

The salt-dried, gold encrusted body of the Great Fifth was enshrined in a golden Buddhist death tower or "chorten." It rises to a height of more than sixty feet through three stories inside the Potala, emerging in a golden finial from the roof of the Palace. Today, three hundred years later, it still stands in the Temple of Sacrifice which is a section of the West Main Hall. The "chortens" or stupas of seven other Dalai Lamas (the Seventh through Thirteenth), also stand in the Potala. The tomb of the Sixth Dalai Lama, who fell into disrepute because of his worldly ways, was conspicuously missing.

The stupas vary in size but are similar

in shape. Derived from Indian prototypes, they have bulbous domes rising from square bases and are surmounted by cone-like masts. All were covered with gold and studded with jade of the purest green, stunning turquoise, rare pink and red corals, diamonds as big as human eyeballs, exotic lapis lazuli, slabs of purple amethyst and blood red rubies. It is recorded that 110,000 taels of gold were used on the chorten of the Great Fifth and that the inlaid jewels were worth ten times more.

This stupa is not quite as resplendent as the tomb of Thupten-gyatso, the Thirteenth Dalai Lama, who died in 1933 at the age of fifty-seven. His spectacular sepulcher, towering seventy feet high, is covered with gold over a solid silver base. The pure gold cone, starting from the rounded middle section where the body is entombed, rises into a forest of silk hangings, rustling brocade thankas and white scarves dangling down like stalactites. The top is surmounted by a bell delicately engraved with the rising sun and waning moon. It is said that the most precious re-

Hall of Western Sunshine.

Buddhist symbols on the roof of the Potala.

lics were buried inside the chortens. Before each tomb stands an altar loaded with golden lamps, silver bowls and other sacrificial vessels. Around each sepulcher are hosts of jewel-encrusted golden Buddhas and fierce protectors.

We looked in wonder at this dazzling display of treasure that was completely unguarded. Presently I seemed to sense the presence of shadowy apparitions, but I was not sure if this eerie mausoleum of the Dalai Lamas was haunted or if I was just experiencing the "strange phenomena" that Mr. Ke had warned us was normal in Tibet. When I told Top of these strange vibes, he laughed and assured me that it was only the altitude. But, if any place deserves to be haunted, it is the Potala. For amid the splendor of its myriad golden Buddhas set in a labyrinth of sacred chambers, there have occurred more rich pageantry and arcane prophecies; more secret ceremonies and magic rituals; more sinister intrigue and mysterious happenings than the imagination can encompass.

Before reaching the Temple of Sacrifice we had climbed from the terrace up dark stairways and through a winding corridor to the East Main Hall where a host of golden images were spaced among sixty-four decorative pillars. This was the largest hall in the White Palace and was used for coronations or "assumption of office," when and if the Dalai Lamas reached the age of majority.

The story of the successor to the Great Fifth, the Sixth Dalai Lama, who disappeared at the age of twenty-three, is revealing of the human contradictions besetting Lamaism. Although his name, Tsang-yang Gyatso, meant "Melodious Purity," he was called by some the "Merry One." Others more bluntly denounced him as dissolute and debauched because he boldly strayed from the path of celibacy and virtue. The Sixth built the "House of the Serpent" in the lake below the Potala as a retreat where he could indulge earthly pleasures — wine, women and song — without desecrating the holy precincts of the Potala. It is interesting that his unpriestly behavior was not condemned by ordinary Tibetans who, in their compassion, theorized that the living Buddha had two bodies, one of which stayed in the Potala, meditating, while the other roamed Lhasa, drank chang, the local wine, and made passionate love in the brothels. Later, in honor of the holy visitor, the houses he frequented were washed with yellow, the color associated with purity.

Another explanation given of the behavior of the "Living God" was that the character and earthly inclinations had already been formed by the time he was discovered to be the incarnation of the Buddha, Lord of Compassion. Unlike the other incarnations, who were chosen as infants, the Sixth was already a grown boy, since the death of the Fifth had been concealed for ten years. The next incarnate was assumed to have been born at the moment of the preceeding Dalai Lama's death.

There is yet another explanation Thubten Norbu, brother of the present Dalai Lama (himself believed to be the twenty-fourth reincarnation of a famous Lama, Tagster) gives in his book, *Tibet*. It is also revealing of the tensions within Tibetan Lamaism which tolerated tantric sexual rituals practised in secret by the high monks who had vowed celibacy. It should be noted, however, that although the Sixth assumed the office of Dalai Lama, he was never ordained as a full Lama monk and therefore never took celibacy vows. Norbu wrote:

"It seems possible that the young Tsangyang was initiated into tantric practices which involve physical, rather than mental, sexual intercourse with women. There are various degrees of this, all of which rest in the belief that a vital force is both physical and spiritual . . .

"There is no doubt that the young Tsangyang (the Sixth Dalai Lama) had all the physical urges of any youth when he entered monastic life. We can also be sure that his instructors, headed by his tutor, the Panchen Rinpoche (Panchen Lama),

will have done everything in their power to lead him away from purely physical pleasures, and for this reason it is even more likely that he may have been initiated into tantric practices that would divert his physical desires into spiritual channels."

The stories surrounding the death of the Sixth were as controversial as was his life. Most historians record that he was kidnapped by the Mongols who had openly criticized the young Lama's behavior. They invaded the Potala, are said to have killed the Regent Sanggye-Gyatso, who had concealed the death of the Fifth, and to have taken the Sixth away. It is not known if he died or was murdered. Official records say he died in exile of dropsy.

Another story, told by the brother of the present Dalai Lama, is that the Sixth had a boy child by a special lover with whom he lived in the House of the Serpent. The high monks, afraid the child might inherit the office of Dalai Lama, threw the mother and baby into the Potala dungeons and exiled the "Merry One" to Inner Mongolia where he became the goat herder that legend says he had always longed to be.

Today the sepulcher of the Sixth Dalai Lama is the only one missing from the mausoleum in the Potala. But the young Dalai Lama will always be remembered by Tibetans for the touching and lyrical love poems he left behind. They reveal not only the mental agony of this victim of the system, but the torment of his soul during the painful struggle he waged within himself as to whether he should act like the man he was or the God-king his Regents told him he was. Here is an example translated by Thubten Norbu:

"I went to my teacher, with devotion filled,
To learn of the Lord Buddha.
My teacher taught, but what he said escaped;
For my mind was full of compassion,
Full of that Compassionate One who loves me.
She has stolen my mind." *

---

* Translation from Tibet by Thubten Jigme Norbu, Simon and Schuster, New York

These few lines, from one of his poems translated by Sir Charles Bell, tell of his inner turmoil:

> Dear Love, to whom my heart goes out,
>   If we could but be wed,
> Then had I gained the choicest gem
>   From Ocean's deepest bed.
>
> I chanced to pass my sweetheart fair
>   Upon the road one day;
> A turquoise found of clearest blue
>   Found to be thrown away.
>
> My heart's far off; the nights pass by
>   In sleeplessness and strife;
> E'en day brings not my heart's desire,
>   For lifeless is my life.
>
> I dwell apart in Potala,
>   A god on earth am I;
> But in the town the chief of rogues
>   And boisterous revelry.

After the disappearance of the Sixth Dalai Lama, the country was again plunged into a period of strife with rival monk factions openly fighting for power. In the midst of this a Tartar army mounted on camels invaded Tibet from the plains of Turkestan. The Tibetans again implored China to rescue them. The Emperor Kangshi sent ten thousand mounted warriors to drive out the Tartars. After restoring order in 1720 A.D., the Emperor formally assumed suzerainty over Tibet and appointed two Chinese mandarin officials called Ambans to remain in Lhasa as political overseers. They assumed considerable power and influence over the Regents and had to be consulted on all important decisions including the selection of future Dalai Lamas.

As the theocracy grew stronger and richer, the Lama Regents became reluctant to forfeit their power to the young Dalai Lamas when they reached eighteen years of age. Of the eight Dalai Lamas who succeeded the Sixth, only four lived to assume power. The Seventh, even though he relinquished all political control, died at the age of twenty-three. The Eighth, Ninth and Eleventh died mysteriously before coming

of age and the Tenth died suddenly at twenty-two. The Twelfth survived because he turned over his secular powers to the Regents and went into religious seclusion. Thupten-gyatso, the Thirteenth, was rescued by friends who had discovered a plot to poison him on his eighteenth birthday. He became the first Dalai Lama to exercise the secular and spiritual power of his office for a lifetime; even the Great Fifth had turned over power to his Regent

Door leading to the upper part of the Red Palace.

Ceremonial vessel made of a human skull sits before a royal couch.

in later years. The Thirteenth proved to be a shrewd, energetic figure of considerable political acumen comparable to the Great Fifth. Unfortunately for Tibet, he came to power so long after the monastic theocracy had degenerated and fossilized that, in spite of his admirable efforts, he was unable to bring Tibet out of its stagnation into the twentieth century. The present Fourteenth Dalai Lama was invested with full powers at fifteen, three years under the traditional age, in 1950.

The Dalai Lamas all had their private apartments in the the top part of the Potala where they could be well protected and isolated from earthly temptations. After much climbing we finally entered the Western Sunshine Hall which contains the sacred rooms, prayer halls, shrines, reception rooms and bedrooms of the Dalais, all ornately furnished in golds and brocades but with a certain grimness. One table held a human skull with a silver jaw and silver eyeballs; it stood upside down on a square golden stand supported by human heads made of gold. Beside it was a drum

The official bedroom of the Dalai Lama.

Time has stopped in the bedroom of the Fourteenth Dalai Lama.

64   *Statue of King Songtsen Gampo, with head of the Buddha of Compassion in his turban,*
indicating that he is a reincarnation of the Buddha.

Guardian figure.

One of the royal thrones.

fashioned from human skin stretched over two skulls. They were objects used in some of the elaborate tantric rituals. The walls were covered with bright murals depicting scenes of paradise and the various devils that haunt the eighteen hells of Tibetan Buddhism.

We were not shown the kitchen but Buddhist writer Theos Bernard described it in his book *Penthouse of the Gods;*

"We were led through the kitchen which looked exactly like the old kitchen dramatized by the Baptist in his Hell of fire and damnation. It was about as black and seething a dungeon sweatbox as ever I hoped to pass through in any lifetime."

The Dalai Lama's toilet was a hole in a wooden slab covered with pink velvet. It was rumored that the droppings, which fell four hundred feet below, were carefully collected and made into medicine.

We entered one of the private chapels. As our eyes adjusted to the darkness, we could see the shimmering golden hues of a myriad of jewelled Buddhas of all sizes. Grotesque shadows were cast in the light of a few dim electric bulbs by the figures of wrathful deities, guardian ogres, monsters and fiends protecting the Buddhas. We followed a maze of narrow steps and corridors through room after room of mystic images and symbols that in old Tibet had far more power than reality. They sat silently amidst the wisps of smoke rising like ghosts from bowls of ever-burning yak butter.

At the top of the Palace was the Hall of Sutra where the Dalai Lama would sit on a brocade covered throne to read the scriptures. One of the original sutras brought from India was on display in a glass case. The script had been finely embroidered with gold threads. Other books, wrapped carefully in rich brocades, lined the shelves. Religious books were kept in shelves high on the wall in respect of their sacred character. These scriptures represent the third body, the verbal body of Buddha; the other two being the physical body, represented by images, and the spiritual body, represented by the shrine or mandala. We were told that the libraries in the Potala hold some seven thousand volumes recording Tibetan culture and religion. These include some original sutras from India which were written on palm leaves.

When we reached the flat roof I felt dizzy from the climb and the rarefied air which at 13,123 feet was even thinner than

in Lhasa. My senses were soon restored by the clear view of the Lhasa valley and the city neatly spread out below us. Incredibly we were surrounded on the roof by a blaze of gold-covered canopies rising from the tombs below and adorned by the eight

Buddhist scriptures in the Hall of Sutras.

Mythical beast guards the apartments of the Dalai Lamas.

The golden rooftops can be seen for miles.

Author on roof of the Potala Palace.

70

From the roof of the Potala can be seen the ruins of Medicine Hill Monastery and Lhasa Valley beyond.

auspicious emblems of Buddhism: the conch shell, love knot (Palbu), umbrella, wheel, prayer banner, two fishes, vase and lotus. Dragons with protruding tongues jutted from the roof corners and large bell-shaped cones embossed with gold lettering of the Holy scriptures decorated the edges. It was from the roof top that the Lamas would blow their twelve foot brass horns to call the people to prayers.

On the hilltop facing the Potala we could see the ruins of Chagpori, the old lamaist medical monastery. The fortress-like monastery once towered majestically on the crest of Iron Hill, with the houses of the lama doctors huddled beside its walls. Cut into the hillside was a steep path where the sick and invalid climbed, seeking miraculous healings. They were simple people, ready to be bled or to swallow bits of paper enscribed with holy incantations reputed to combat the "worms of disease." The monastery overlooked the main road to Lhasa and because of its strategic position became the very center of the fighting during the armed rebellion. It is not known how many were killed, but the monastery was left in ruins.

Looking down we could see the steep cliffs below Red Hill. In the past this was a place of entertainment for the Lamas. Acrobats and serfs risking their lives to pay their debts performed daring rope tricks. Each year, on the second day of the first month of the Tibetan Calender, four leather ropes, over one hundred yards long, were tied and dropped from the roof to a pillar at the foot of the hill. The performer affixed a piece of rawhide to the front of his jacket, which was tied over the rope. Then, suspended from the rope, holding a white flag in each hand, he slid down head first. Even if he survived, once was not enough. If he could repeat this three times, he was exempted from corvee labor for a year. But many were killed in such attempts.

Leaving the Potala we climbed down the stairway to the sprawl of stone houses at the foot of the Palace. Although we had

spent a full afternoon, we had seen only a small part of the great castle. We did not see the dungeons, which, like the rest of the Potala, now stand empty. In old Tibet legal practices were often barbaric. No civil law governed the treatment of the serfs or peasants who were considered property of the landowner. Maiming of limbs, eye gouging and flogging in the public square before being condemned to the dungeons were common punishments for petty and religious crimes despite a decree limiting these methods of punishment to conspirators and traitors.

Lhasa Museum now displays the gruesome instruments of torture found in the prisons of the Potala, according to the Communist authorities. The exhibits include severed hands, pickled human heads, the tanned skins of children said to have been flayed alive as sacrifices, and photos of starved and mutilated victims. The grimest display was the roasted body of a fourteen-year-old girl draped in silks seated on a chair in a glass case. According to our Tibetan guide, a youth of pale aesthetic features, the victim was one of triplet sisters believed by certain sects to have been sired, as were all multiple births, by the devil himself. Practitioners of the occult had, in a demonic ritual, exorcised the devils by roasting the three girls and their "witch mother" to death; thus saving them from the eighteen hells.

The only American known to have actually visited the Potala prison was Theos Bernard, a Buddhist monk, who obtained his Ph.D. at Columbia University. He toured the Potala in 1939 and described it in his book *Penthouse of the Gods*,

"The prison reminded one of a trap to catch a man-eating lion; it was filled with wretched, withered souls, trotting about with shackled limbs. We entered into a conversation with one poor fellow. He told us that he had stolen a couple of charm boxes about five years ago, and he had no idea when he would be released. What actually happens is that the Government forgets whom they had put in and for how

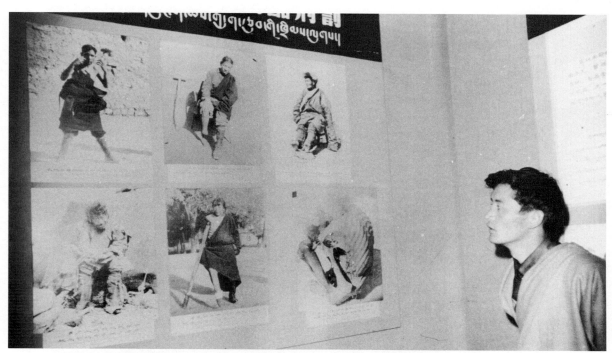

Photos in the Lhasa Museum of victims said to have been found in the dungeons.

Amputation was a common punishment.
Severed hands were found in the prison.

Flayed skins of children.

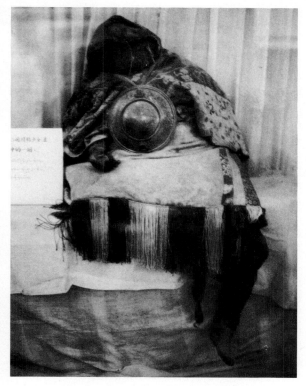

Exorcised body of a young girl, a triplet and
therefore believed to be possessed of devils.

73

long, which means that once in, always in, unless one day the Government decides to win a little grace by releasing some of its prisoners; and on so auspicious a day any man may be the lucky one. Just as we were about to leave, we heard faint echoes which emanated from a still lower dungeon, a crying soul was going through the ritual that he might gain happiness in the next life. It turned out to be a friend of Tharchin's, who had once been very powerful, and had the reputation of being a fine scholar to boot."

Even the ruling class was not safe from the brutalities of Tibetan justice. Theos Bernard goes on to describe the fate of some members of Government during the turmoil following the death of the Thirteenth Dalai Lama: "Some had their eyes gouged out, others their tongues cut out, still others were imprisoned for life . . . The person next in rank to Tsarong (who was in charge of the army), who had the repu-

tation of being one of the best scholars, had his eyes put out; he is now (1939) sitting in a dungeon at the Potala waiting for the end to come." *

It was late afternoon when Top and I returned to the Guest House ready for oxygen "cocktails" to help us revive from our strenuous explorations. From the window we could see the setting sun, now a vermillion disk, just dipping behind the snowy peaks in the West. It beamed its last warming rays on the Potala, swathing the Red Palace in a crimson glow and the pinnacles of the golden funeral towers in a shimmering aura. The sun suddenly dropped. The castle was slowly shrouded in shadows — a spectacular but sinister fantasy, wreathed in the romance of centuries.

* Penthouse of the Gods by Theos Bernard, Charles Scribner's Sons, New York 1939

3. The Rice Heap:
Inside The Drepung Monastery

The Drepung Monastery.

Gargoyles guard the doorways.

The Drepung Monastery is a honeycomb of white stone blocks studded with black framed windows and dark red doorways leading to a maze of chambers, chapels and gloomy cells. The sacred temples above the living quarters are ringed with crimson collars made of inlaid willow branches, pressed together and dyed the same royal color as the Red Palace in the Potala. The whole complex looked like a walled-in medieval city, but still I could see how it derived its name, "the Rice Heap." From a distance it looked like a pile of steamed rice that had been poured over the hillside by a giant hand. Later I learned that it was named after the famous Tantric monastery of India, Sri-Dhanya-Kataka.

The Drepung is the largest of the three great monasteries in Tibet — the other two being the Ganden and Sera — and it was once the largest in the world. At the height of its power and influence, the Drepung housed over 10,000 lamas and student monks, not including the acolytes. The monastery owned about 25,000 serfs who toiled on 185 manorial estates, and 15,000 herdsmen who worked the 300 pastures. In 1959 when the monastery was taken over, the serfs were indebted to it for a total of 140,000 tons of grain and 10 million yuan (approximately $5 million) which would have taken generations to repay. It also controlled 700 subsidiary monasteries. In October 1979 there were only 270 lamas and no student monks in the Drepung.

We came by car. About five miles west of Lhasa we turned north off the main road and began to ascend a green wooded slope toward the monastery. The road ended immediately below the Drepung near

PHOTO RIGHT: The golden doorknocker is embossed with Buddhist symbols.

The Chanting Hall of the main temple.

Repairing the monastery.

Nechung, a group of white buildings nestled in a lush grove where the State Oracle once resided and where the bodies of former oracles are entombed in shrines.

Oracles and prophets played an unofficial but important role in the old theocratic government of Tibet. Many decisions of state were based on the prognostications of these soothsayers. The nation's chief seer was the Natchung Oracle who, once every month, in a ceremony as bizarre as the Lama Theocracy itself, would go into a cataleptic trance and peer into the future to guide official actions. To my knowledge Theos Bernard, who was himself an ordained Buddhist monk, is the only Westerner to have witnessed this ceremony when he visited Tibet in 1939. I quote at length from his book, *Penthouse of the Gods*, because it gives a unique insight into Tibetan religious ceremonies.

"The oracle came in, dressed in a gorgeous array of yellow brocade, with a sort of witch-hat. He seated himself Buddha-fashion, on the floor in front of his throne. Four men held him in a mood of greatest tension, as if to be ready for the moment the spirit made his entrance; for them, the oracle was no longer a human being, but the recipient of the spirit's confidence, and its spokesman. While he sat there in silent meditation, in order to relax his nerves and yield to whatsoever manner of convulsion this never-ending din would induce, two rows of drums continued their beating on one side, while on the other side trumpets went on with their unceasing blast; at the same time about thirty seated monks were chanting their sacred formula. At last he began to quiver, and the drummers and trumpeters drew closer and closer to him with an increasing volume of mystic sounds, finally drumming and blowing directly into the ears of the oracle in order to prevail upon him to stay. After an hour of this unceasing rhythm — even I could not resist it and felt my emotions merge with the vibrations of the room — the spirit must have entered the oracle, for he began to vibrate like a G-string on a base viol,

while his four attendants were trying to hold him down. His strength grew terrific, and they were forced to yield in the end, content merely to keep hold of him to prevent bodily injury. With this he suddenly sprung from the floor, still in his cross-legged position, far above the heads of all in the room. He repeated this several times. Then he straightened out and stood

Gandun Gyatso, The Oracle Monk.

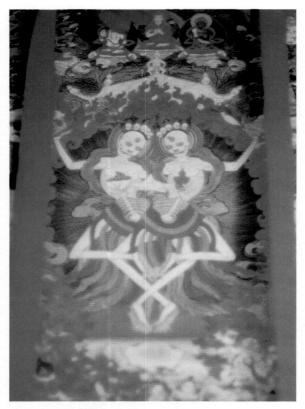

Dancing skeletons.

up, pacing the floor back and forth before ascending the throne reserved for the Dalai Lama. During this exercise he appeared to be keeping time, and made a strange sort of noise very much like a hiccough. Then he made way to his throne, where several cups of some kind of drink were offered him; he consumed it like an accomplished heavy drinker. An attendant held a large number of short red scarves, which the priests placed around the neck of those making offerings to him. A congested line of Lamas formed; they held the katas (long silk scarves) in readiness to offer them to him as soon as they could work their way to his feet. During all this time he continued his hiccoughing noise, and reciting whatever the spirit would impart during the emotional fit. Persons from all over the place were rushing to the windows to witness the scene. Shortly he spotted the onlookers and, reaching for a silver cup and anything else that came to hand, he flung them in their direction with the splenetic fury of a hysterical wife or husband.

"Thus, I had come to witness one of the

Detail of religious thanka showing lamas of the Gelupka sect (Yellow hats) above.
Below, are fierce gods, Mahakala, dancing in an aura of flames and crushing victims beneath their feet.

greatest spectacles of all Tibet."

The incoherent noises that came from the oracle during his fit were only decipherable by the chief ministers who then advised the Regent or Dalai Lama. If the advice proved to be wrong, the oracle was blamed, suitably punished and replaced.

One of the Chief Lamas of Drepung Monastery now lives in the Oracle's shrine. His name was Gandun Gyatso but I called him the Oracle Monk. Wrapped in his crimson robes he came towards us in short mincing steps, toes pointing outwards. I was immediately smitten by his yellow yak-hide boots curled at the toes like Chinese roof corners. The palms of his hands were pressed together in the traditional Buddhist greeting. When he smiled he looked disarmingly debonair with his even white teeth framed by a thin brush of black whiskers. His whole appearance, just as the hewn rock stairway leading to the monastery, presented an impression of eternal Tibet.

He led us upwards. Slowly, slowly we climbed, inching our way through slippery cobblestone canyons banked on both sides with whitewashed dormitories and two-storied stone houses where the high lamas once lived with their acolytes. Soon we were gasping for breath in the rarefied atmosphere while the sympathetic monks waited patiently, urging us to take it slowly.

Finally we came to a great red door in a stone wall. The oracle monk pushed it open. It creaked in protest. We found ourselves on a rock-paved terrace before the wine and gold colored chanting hall of the main temple. This is where all the monks from the four colleges that made up the monastery would gather for sunrise mass. The smallest and most exclusive of these colleges was the one devoted to the study of Tantra.

In Tibet, the Tantric teachings of the Indian mystic Padma Sambharu were subject to varied interpretations and often to great abuse when practised by unqualified monks. In an effort to avoid this, participa-

Esoteric tantric statue symbolizing the union of a deity and consort.

83

tion in Tantric ritual and entrance to the erotic Tantric shrines were supposedly limited to lamas who had devoted years of study to the sutras or were incarnate Buddhas, but this rule was often overlooked.

The followers of Tantra were mostly from the "black" and "red" hat sects. They proceeded on the theory that understanding is developed through experience. Thus, followers were permitted a measure of worldliness including women, marriage and wine. For non-Buddhists, Tantra is the most incomprehensible and esoteric of all Buddhist sects. Its doctrine and rituals fill eighteen volumes containing an encyclopedia of ancient wisdom as well as essays on spiritual science and yoga. Yet, with all this written guidance, it was still considered beyond intellectual understanding; the truth could only be perceived by intuition. The key to the ultimate knowledge could only be given by the "master" to his "initiate" who was sworn to secrecy.

In simple terms, however, it was a kind of short cut to Nirvana, even though it took a lifetime of study. Practitioners believed if they persevered with severe intensity they could achieve Buddhahood in one lifetime, thus escaping the "Wheel of Life" or the endless cycle of reincarnation. The central asumption is that "kundalini energy" or the essence of Buddhahood (Christians might call it soul or God) lies within themselves as does the power to obtain it. The difficulty is to find the correct pathway to reach this Buddhahood. In a sense the seeker must journey inside himself and attempt to reintegrate with his own divine essence. It is a complicated and multi-layered road which involves the use of "Mantra," mystical words; "Mandala," sacred diagrams; and "Shakti," female deities. The rituals include the use of wine, meat, meditation on corpses and spiritual or physical sexual intercourse which symbolically unites activity (female) and wisdom (male).

It was believed that the "absolute truth" of Tantra would reveal itself gradually and only to the high prelates who were be-

lieved to have already achieved divine status through previous incarnations. The ordinary, illiterate believers were only permitted access to a "relative truth" which basically required blind faith in the "Three Gems": Buddha, the law of Buddha and the monkhood. This could lead to Nirvana only through future reincarnations.

Tantric rituals are symbolized in the temples by erotic statues of wrathful Gods. In the Drepung the chief Tantric deity was Dorge Jig-je, who was represented as a "Yidam" or fiend with a monster's head and sixteen arms holding his female counterpart, or "Dakini," in sexual embrace under a ring of leaping flames.

When we stepped over the threshold into the main hall which was dimly lit with flickering yak-butter lamps, we could see these "Yidams" along the walls and around the main images. They seemed to be used as guardians. The male, usually black, was decorated with human skulls while the female was in hues of red. The figures were invariably draped in silks showing only the heads, arms and feet which were dancing on the writhing bodies of humans and animals. The imagery of Tantra is often so obscured with the magic and supernatural symbols of Bön that it confounds human understanding.

The awesome chanting hall, built in 1416 A.D., is supported by rows of pillars hung with brocade strips. The walls are completely covered with embroidered thankas and paintings of deities, various Buddhas and the sixteen disciples. Three giant golden Buddhas representing the Past, Present and Future were seated along one wall surrounded by a host of smaller deities all encrusted with sparkling gems.

It was only one of scores of halls, chapels and shrines in the Drepung. Each new generation of rulers added their own private shrines. We explored dozens of such gloomy sanctuaries packed with galaxies of gold and jeweled images.

Chenresik, Buddha of Compassion.

Statue of a Living Buddha meditating.

next reincarnation. The whole thing is a crime against nature. The insurmountable ego of the human animal must find a way to rise to power, and in Tibet the easiest avenue which leads to the greatest power is that of religion. It is about the only avenue where those on their glorified thrones do not have to offer something to the suffering downtrodden people who

Like all the other monasteries, the Drepung was supported by the lay people. The ruling abbots had the right to levy taxes on everything from yaks to haircuts. Altogether there were forty-five different taxes. The abbots also amassed great riches from other sources, including religious ceremonies, estate revenues, trade and money lending. The wealth squeezed from the poor and accumulated in the monasteries had an essentially evil influence which tainted the spiritual purity of Tibetan Buddhism.

The riches, however, were seldom used for the personal comforts of the lamas, but rather were poured into the decoration of the monastery which symbolized power. One can only begin to imagine the extent of the treasures stored in these fortress-like temples of Tibet. The abundance of wealth, however, reflected a general corruption so deep that even the most sympathetic visitors in the past were shocked and repulsed.

The American Buddhist monk, Theos Bernard, noted how the monasteries had deviated from the teachings of Buddha:

. . . *"Here were the pillars of their society to which all must submit. You begin to wonder how such simple people could ever raise such walls of glory. Their beauty was erected centuries ago by the call of faith, evolving the hope of escape in the*

Statue of the Great Fifth, who was once an abbot of the Drepung, rises above images of previous abbots.

have been their means to power . . . Are these the conceptions and teachings of Buddha? NO! . . . I beheld the magnificence of the jewelled altars of gold protected by the glittering deities of the faith, representing the suppression of the intelligence over centuries."

Nevertheless, standing amid the awesome display of benevolent and wrathful Gods, I began to understand how the lamas were able to wield a power so frightening over the superstitious and poverty-stricken masses that they were able to make time stand still for three hundred years. What was more perplexing was that the faithful flock had been so enthralled or intimidated that they were willing to die of starvation in order that still another jewel could adorn a lifeless idol in the local monastery.

There are chapels in the Drepung dedicated to the first five Dalai Lamas, and their images stand as large and glittering as the statues of Buddha. The Drepung was the stronghold of the Gelupka ("Yellow Hats") until the Great Fifth united Tibet and moved into the Potala in 1653.

The rooms in the Drepung occupied by the Great Fifth while he was building the Potala have been preserved as have the golden death chortens of the early Dalai Lamas. The first three Dalai Lamas were abbots of the Drepung. The third, Sonamgyatso (1543-88) was actually the first to hold the title of Dalai Lama, meaning Ocean of Wisdom. But when the title was bestowed on him by the Mongol King Altan Khan of the Tumeds in 1578, the previous two deceased abbots became Dalai Lamas retroactively or posteriori. The succeeding or fourth Dalai Lama, Yontengyatso (1589-1617) was a grandson of Altan Khan, thus linking again the destinies of the Tibetans and Mongols.

All Tibetan monasteries have a Temple of the Guardian of the Law which is kept very dark. The walls of the passageway and the chapel walls are covered with frescoes depicting scenes of death and mutilated corpses. Deities in their most fearsome aspects are seen dancing on parts of bodies — the intestines, heart and eyes — all the things, according to historian Thubten Norbu, "that the lesser tantrists, by taking them literally instead of symbolically, have abused, misleading themselves and others."

The function of these hellish shrines was to teach the truth of impermanence and suffering. "The force of destruction itself," says Norbu, "can be turned to good ends when it is directed against evil . . . We should leave the temple filled only with compassion for all suffering."

Besides the 200,000 monks in old Tibet, there were about 3,000 nuns who were headed by an Abbess known as the "Thunderbolt Sow" or the Pig-faced Abbess. She was believed to be a sorceress and a living incarnation of the she-devil Palden Lhamo (in Hindu, Kali) who, with her consort Tamdin, defended Buddhism against its enemies. She was respected by all Buddhist sects, although she belonged to the "red-hatted" Nyingma sect and shared the royal privilege of riding in a sedan chair with the Dalai Lama, the Regent and the two Chinese Mandarin Ambans. There were also a few monasteries where monks and nuns lived together, and all of their children were given to the monastery.

Not all Tibetan monks lived in monasteries; some retired to hermitages and some fanatics or saints, depending on one's outlook, lived in voluntary imprisonment, immured in a living tomb with no light. Such a man had only a rosary of human bones, a trumpet made of a human thigh bone to signal if he wanted out and the top of a human skull to eat out of. The only worldly communication was made when he reached out through a peephole to get daily food. In 1903 a British Army officer and Tibetan scholar, L. Austine Waddell, visited "The Cave of Happy Musings on Misery" where he saw the hand of an old hermit who had been holed up for twenty-one years. In his book *Lhasa and Its Mysteries* he gives this chilling description:

"Whilst we were standing outside and pitying the poor man who voluntarily pent himself up in this prison, one of us asked to be shown evidence of the hermit's presence inside. Thereupon the attendant gave the signal which they use when they deposit the food. He tapped very gently thrice on the sill, so softly that it was almost inaudible to us, and then, after ten or twelve seconds, whilst we held our breath expectantly, in a silence like that of the tomb, the tiny rabbit-hutch door in front of us trembled, then began to move and was jerkily pushed ajar about three inches or so, and from the deep gloom came slowly falthering forth A GLOVED HAND! This was all. Only a gloved hand! It protruded about four inches onto the stone-slabbed sill and slowly fumbled there for two or three seconds, and finding nothing, it returned slowly, trembling into its shell, and nothing broke the agonizing silence save, as I fancied, a suppressed moan. The whole action was muffled like a dream, so slow, so stealthy, so silent and creepy. In the daylight it was unearthly and horrible to a degree. Only a gloved hand! So the stimulus of light even was denied to the poor wretch's hand, another drop in the cup of his misery. It was difficult to realize that a human being could be so confined voluntarily; it was only fit for a caged wild beast."

The purpose of this masochistic meditation was to conquer all desire and exorcise all devils in this life and thus come closer to Nirvana in the next incarnation. Some hermits who died while voluntarily incarcerated were believed to have attained Buddahood.

From the golden roof top of the Drepung, we had a panoramic view of the valley below, green and threaded with streams flowing into the Lhasa River. At the foot of the hill directly below us was a cluster of buildings where the butchering was done for the lamas. It was known as "skin-flag" because it was the place in earlier centuries where the heretics and the disobedient were executed. Their skins

In the library sacred Buddhist scriptures are wrapped in brocade.

were made into flags which were flown in the wind to warn others.

The story of the changes that have occurred in the monasteries since 1959 is linked closely to all Tibetan society, for the monasteries were the "pillars of the state."

Before the abrupt and wide-sweeping social transformation carried out by the Communists, Tibetan society was so dominated by the monkhood that almost every aspect of life from birth to marriage, illness and death, required the prayers, ceremonial rituals and scriptural guidance of the local lamas.

Lama doctors and exorcists spent a major part of their time preparing amulets and charms to cure illnesses and drive out evil spirits. By far the most important time requiring the presence of Lamas was during death and funerals. Funeral ceremonies were arranged, among other things, to fill the treasuries of the monasteries. If the deceased was too poor to pay for prayers, he was fed to the river, but if the survivors gave sufficient offerings for a ceremony and forty-nine days of prayer, the monks would assist the dead into a better life in

PHOTO LEFT: Monsters decorated with skulls symbolize the horror of the eighteen hells.

Terrifying guardians protect the Buddhas.

the next incarnation. Wealthy families were required to donate to the poor as well as give a large sum to the monastery, the interest of which would pay for a prayer each year.

At the moment of death, the presiding lama would pluck a hair from the top of the dead man's head to release his spirit. Then, after a period of time, the body was tied into the fetus position and carried up a mountain where it was laid out and dismembered by specialists. The flesh was stripped off and fed to the vultures, and the bones were pulverized, mixed with wheat flour and spread out for smaller carrion to eat. Thus, according to the lamas, even in death the body could be of use to fellow creatures. The family always attended this ceremony to insure that the thigh bones and skulls were not taken by Tantric sects for use in secret rituals unless the astrologer, who was always consulted, recommended they be employed in this manner. The bodies of the high lamas were often cremated or, as in the case of the incarnate Buddhas, buried in the lotus position.

In Tibet, special scriptures called Bardo-thodrol were devoted to the art of dying. It was believed that the appropriate death was the sole purpose of living, and it was considered more important than birth. The period between death and rebirth was called "Bardo." There were seven stages through Bardo and each stage was subdivided into seven steps (seven was a sacred number). The forty-nine days of prayer, therefore, represented the seven times seven stages of Bardo.

Only the lamas were believed to possess the wisdom to guide the dead safely through these terrible stages, and this was the main reason for the existence of such a large monkhood. The strength of the Tibetan theocracy lay in the ritual and occult powers of the monasteries. Monks were the only literate people and only they could read the scriptures and explain the Law of Life to the people. Although lama scholars knew nothing of western medi-

cine, science, arts or literature, they mastered the esoteric aspects of Tantra and the obscure Buddhist sutras translated from Indian. Their knowledge of ancient rituals, meditation, the art of yoga and metaphysics was unique in Tibet. Not surprisingly, they saw no reason to jeopardize the effect of their mystic power by permitting lay education.

Contemporary Tibetan historians estimate that as late as the 1950's at least one out of every four able-bodied men belonged to the monkhood. This statistic did not include the thousands of small boys given to the monasteries to escape abject poverty and insure a religious education. Although discipline was severe and many monks served as slaves to high lamas or had to beg for alms, they were at least guaranteed a livelihood.

The monkhood was forcibly dismantled after the Lama theocracy came tumbling down in 1959. In an elaborate reception room in the Drepung Monastery we drank rich, yak-butter tea and chatted with the Oracle Monk about the past. He poured tea from a thermos bottle and told us he had been born in Inner Mongolia sixty-two years ago. He had entered a monastery at the age of seven and at eighteen he became obsessed with a desire to see the holy city of Lhasa and to study Tibetan Buddhism. He walked, alone, for over a year, through freezing rains and snow up to his knees. He survived on wild plants and food begged from nomads and other pilgrims. He said he had never regretted his decision and was still a devout Buddhist.

What happened to the other monks?

We were informed that the Drepung and the seven hundred subsidiary monasteries had been centers of resistance during the armed insurrection in 1959. Guns and other weapons had been smuggled into the monastery and stored amid the sacred images. There were about fifty-six hundred monks in the monastery at that time.

Reception room in the Drepung.

94

The author with the Chief Lamas in the Drepung.

Silk tapestry paying homage to Chairman Mao Zedong.

Besides five hundred high lama leaders, about four thousand monk soldiers were actively involved in the resistance. After the rebellion had been crushed in Lhasa by the Peoples Liberation Army (PLA), the troops marched into the monasteries. They met little resistance among the monks who were left in the Drepung itself because about three thousand activists had already fled to India to be near the Dalai Lama or joined the Khampa guerrilla resistance.

The PLA told the monks they could return to their homes and farm the land, work on roads or construction projects, or remain as working monks in the monastery. Resisters were arrested and most of the monasteries' land was confiscated. About 50 acres of orchards and fields were left to the Drepung. Besides caring for the temples, the 270 monks who chose to stay in their cloisters earn a living by tending their 12,000 fruit trees. They can sell the fruit privately or to the State. They also grow chingko barley and care for over a thousand sheep, milk cows and yaks. The oldest monk is 83 and the youngest 30. Those too old to work are supported by the State which allots 3 million yuan a year for the upkeep and repair of the monastery. Most of the carpentry and mason work is done by monks or former monks. Indeed it seemed that most of the men we met in Tibet were self-defrocked monks. Surprisingly, none expressed bitterness about the fate of the monasteries. The monks that remained seem to have accepted their lot with Buddhist fatalism. In the Drepung, the Oracle Monk told us that he worked from early morning until 4:30 in the afternoon. "Then I rest and pray and read sutras."

"What do you think about the changes?" I asked.

"I am not sad because the Lamas have

decreased — some died, some took part in the revolt, some went to prison or escaped and went home. Others married and live in the vicinity or went to work in government offices. They can no longer live off the work of others." He gave us a resigned smile and picked up his tea glass in both hands. "Now the life of the people is much better." He sipped his tea loudly, put down his glass and smoothed his crimson robes. "Our life is better, too," he added.

The sun was already low in the sky when we took our leave. We thanked the monks and had one last look at some of the priceless works of sacred art they so conscientiously cared for. We were led back to the big red door where a litter of fat kittens were playing on a ladder. The Oracle Monk reached out to stroke a little gray one as we passed by. The kitten followed him through the gate and down the steep descent to the foot of the hill where our car was waiting. The monks waved until we were out of sight.

Long afterwards I could feel the warmth and strength of these gentle men of unerring faith who had survived not only the tyranny of the high Lamas but sometimes harsh reforms of the Communists.

Stone stairway leads past the dormitory buildings.

97

4. Lhasa: Old And New

The crowded main thoroughfare of old Lhasa.

Bicycles are the principal transportation in Lhasa.

Old Lhasa is a quaint maze of circular, cobblestone streets lined with two- and three-storied houses made of stone blocks and oblong, sun-baked bricks in typical Trans-himalayan style. Like the Potala, the walls of the buildings were tapered slightly inward with narrow, inset windows, wider at the base. They were framed with black paint and more often than not the deep sills were loaded with carefully tended flowers which in Tibet convey both beauty and spirituality, as they are symbols of the Buddha. The wooden doors were painted in a variety of gay colors which added to the cheerful affect.

We had been invited to visit Mr. Denba, who was the head of a Neighborhood Committee. In 1960 the old city had been cleaned up and divided into neighborhoods supervised by committees who encouraged all citizens to share responsibility, keep their area clean and to participate in social and political activities. The neighborhood was located in the middle of old Lhasa. The streets were filled with good natured people in colorful costumes.

Faces of Lhasa.

Faces of Lhasa.

Faces of Lhasa.

Some were from other places in China, but most of the Han Chinese live in another area of the city called new Lhasa while the Tibetans reside in old Lhasa.

The women looked full of vigor, in their striped aprons which were worn over long dark tunics and brilliant blouses; most of them glowed with rosy mountain complexions. The teenage girls tended to wear long strings of beads and favor wide-brimmed hats worn at a tilt, while the adult women braided their thick hair with silken threads and wound it around their

PHOTO RIGHT: View from the Denba's apartment.

heads in a becoming manner. The men sported a variety of jaunty headgear at odd angles. Some of the hats were fur-lined and worn with one ear flap half down, others looked like western cowboy or Mexican hats. Many of the men had high cheek bones and wide faces that resembled those of American Indians. Hair and whiskers seemed to sprout out in all directions.

The streets contained a mix of Han Chi-

Mrs. Denba, wife of the leader of the Neighborhood Committee, on her balcony.

nese in cotton suits, local city folk in quality yak-wool and strapping country bumpkins who were distinguishable by their greasy, fur-lined robes with knives and flint bags girdled to their bright sashes. The more flamboyant of these yokels bared one shoulder to the cold leaving the long empty sleeve dangling nonchalantly around their heavy boots as they swaggered along the street looking like characters in search of an opera.

The thing that struck me most was that nothing was symmetrical in Lhasa. Not the sloping buildings, nor the streets or hats, or costumes; even people's heads. No two sides ever looked quite the same. Even the Potala, which could be seen towering in the distance from every part of Lhasa, had asymmetric towers like a giant pipe organ. But somehow a strange balance, even a unity, was achieved.

The Denbas lived in a bright, three-room apartment on the second floor of a block of buildings surrounding a large common courtyard. We were invited to sit around a tea table with our host, Mr. Denba, who wore a blue Chinese jacket and gripped a long, black cigarette holder between his yellow teeth. His face was dry and wrinkled beyond his forty years. During most of our conversation he was lost in billows of smoke which he coughed up like an energetic steam engine. He explained that there were about six hundred families in the neighborhood divided into fifteen groups. His neighborhood had organized a handicraft cooperative of eight trades: shoemakers, tailors, leathermakers, carpenters, stones masons, builders, carpet makers and blacksmiths.

Before the reforms that began in the sixties, the people of old Lhasa were divided into three main social stratas, each embracing several classes. On high were the incarnate Buddhas, the abbots of the monasteries, regents and high prelates. In the same strata, but somewhat lower, came the monks and nobles who were government officials. Then the monks and nobles engaged in the import-export trade and

other successful commercial activities. The main branches of Tibetan trade were monopolized by the big monasteries and a few wealthy families.

The next strata, far below, consisted of the local traders, the merchant class, mule suppliers and the craftsmen, such as weavers, printers, carpenters, potters, gold and silver smiths, stone masons, tailors and cooks. On the bottom were the outcasts that even doctors were forbidden to treat; these were the blacksmiths and people who worked with iron, the butchers who were mostly Muslims and the disposers of the dead. Then there were the beggars and released criminals in shackles who were in a category of their own.

"My father was a blacksmith," said Denba, "and so was I. We were the lowest of lows. People used to call us 'black bones.' They thought that even the bones of a blacksmith were black. I could not even earn enough money to eat."

His wife poured thick, yak-butter tea into cups and urged us to drink. We smiled and raised our cups to our lips with both hands.

"Look at me now," said Denba waving away some smoke. "I'm head of the Neighborhood Committee. I have a nice place to live, like my neighbors."

It was true. The rooms were light and well furnished with carpets and lacquer chests. The walls and ceiling were covered with flowered wallpaper. Paper flowers hung from the rafters beside a photo of former Premier Zhou En-lai. A bed in the corner was piled high with woolen blankets and sheepskins.

"My wife and I earn over 150 yuan a month," he went on. "I have a son in the PLA and a daughter at school. I never had the chance to go to school, but now I am learning to read the newspapers. In the old society we couldn't change our lives. We had to stay in the class we were born into. It was our fate. Now we can learn any trade we want so trade has developed rapidly. The workers earn from 3 yuan ($2) per day to 1½ yuan ($1) per day, depending

Mrs. Denba serving yak-butter tea.

knees was a crime. They had to speak to their superiors in whispers and hold their hands over their mouths, lest their vile breath contaminate the air. This they accepted as their unchangeable destiny.

"The Neighborhood Committee is elected by the residents and approved by the Street Office," said Denba. "For big decisions we confer with the Ba Joy Street Office Committee which has four neighborhoods under it. Old Lhasa has three Street Offices."

Mrs. Denba hovered nearby. Her hair was braided up with blue silk. She smiled constantly and never took her eyes off our tea cups. As soon as we took a sip she hurried to pour more. If we took too long between sips she picked up the cup herself, put it to our lips and poured the rich, rancid tea down our throats. Tibetan hospitality was truly overwhelming.

"Could we visit some of your neighbors? " I asked.

They took us next door to see Lan Ge a thirty-two-year-old shoemaker and his thirty-year-old wife, Sa Mu, who worked in a hat factory. He made 80 Yuan ($60) per month and she made 74 Yuan. They had two healthy, young children who attended primary school and lived in a three-room apartment plus kitchen. Everything was splashed with color, the ceiling was hung with pink cloth and the walls were flow-

on the work and technique. We stick to the principle of 'to each according to his work.' When a man is too old to work, the cooperative helps the family, but it is still difficult for them. In the old society many of these trade people were only beggars. In those days we could not even make our own matches; now we can make everything we need."

He paused to cough. Then he explained how the committee arranges wedding celebrations, patches up family quarrels and works out ways of improving production and raising living standards.

In the old society blacksmiths, like our host Denba and other people of inferior rank, dared not take their eyes off the road when the aristocrats and high lamas passed by, for to look above their noble

ered. Dragon carpets were spread on the beds and benches and carved chests lined the walls. A parafin hot plate stood on the kitchen counter.

"Who does the cooking?" I asked.

"I do," said the wife.

"But you work all day too. Doesn't your husband help you?"

She threw her head back and laughed harshly. He looked at her sharply. She swallowed and looked at him sideways. "A little," she said.

In the past each class had its own marriage and sexual customs. The women from the two hundred noble families had considerable freedom and influence. They could own property and ride about on horse-back wherever they pleased, dressed in their furs and silks with high jewelled headresses and dripping with turquoise, the good luck stone. Their marriages were arranged by the parents and divorce was fairly easy if both sides agreed. A man could have any number of concubines and often married all the sisters of one family.

Among the lower classes and serfs there were no marriage ceremonies and consequently no responsibilities. A man could abandon his family when it was convenient to do so. Household slaves and women of the 'black bones' and other outcasts had no rights. They could be used at will, raped or otherwise abused by their masters and roving monks. If a woman complained about 'rape against her will,' she was further punished by having to pay a fine of one silver coin. If she had 'consented to rape,' she had to pay three silver coins. All sexual sins were attributed to the woman. She was not allowed to touch the clothing of a Lama. No wonder the women of the lower classes were such enthusiastic defenders of the democratic reforms which raised their status.

"What do you do for amusement?" I asked.

The husband answered, "Off duty I play basketball, but we prefer the movies."

"What kind?"

"We have Chinese and foreign films. We take the children. It costs 20¢. The last film we saw was the American film 'Convoy.' We also saw 'Future World,' a science fiction film with Chinese dubbed in."

"How did you like it?"

Lan Ge adjusted his glasses and his eyes lit up. "We got the impression that the U.S. is very advanced in technology."

"Would you like to go?"

"Yes, very much!"

"We hope you will be able to visit us in New York one day."

The wife took both my hands in hers. "I had no father, my mother was a beggar but look at what I have. New York is far away, but I hope so."

On the way out we were unexpectedly taken to see another interesting neighbor. The door was opened by a white-jacketed man of refined appearance who ushered us, with a sweep of his arm, into an inner room. The walls had been painted bright orange like the reception room of a monastery. There, on a carpeted couch, was a courtly old Lama named Lunzhutachi, reclining in the lotus position. He was robed in scarlet and saffron and looked exactly like the Living Buddha he indeed was. At the age of eight he had been discovered to be a divine reincarnation by the Chief Abbot of Sera Monastery. He was taken to the monastery, given religious training and eventually made a high prelate.

He smiled serenely and motioned us to sit down. We asked about his childhood.

"When I was young and small in the monastery," he recalled, "I wanted to play, but the teachers were very strict with me. But the feeling between the chief Lama and myself was still good."

We asked him how he survived the armed rebellion in 1959.

"I didn't take part in the revolt," he said, "but my younger brother did. He was imprisoned for ten years and released because of ill health, but he died soon after at the age of seventy-one."

Lama Lunzhutachi, like a number of other Living Buddhas in Lhasa, now holds a well paid position as a "democratic per-

Living Buddha, Lunzhutachi, formerly from Sera Temple, now has his own apartment in Denba's neighborhood.

Hospital of Tibetan Medicine in Lhasa.

sonage" and member of the Political Consultant Congress, which is an organization of prominent, non-Communist Tibetans who cooperate with the Communist regime. He earns the equivalent of U.S. $119 a month, about twice the salary of a factory foreman.

The monk owned one of the apartments in Denba's neighborhood, which he rented out except for the three rooms he lived in himself, with what appeard to be his two servants. Behind a curtained door off his bedroom was a storeroom stacked high with carved chests and other exquisite antique furniture which he said he had brought with him from the monastery. Conspicuously missing from his decorative rooms were any images of Buddha, but there were paper flowers in porcelain vases and scenic photos of the Imperial Palace and Temple of Heaven in Peking. There was also a small photo of Chairman Hua Guofeng.

When asked if he still gave spiritual guidance, the Lama said he did not teach religion, but some neighbors still came to him for personal advice.

By the time we took our leave it seemed that all of the forty thousand people in old Lhasa had come to see the people from another world. We descended a stairway leading into a courtyard jammed with friendly faces, but it was like stepping into quicksand. In their excitement the rather grubby, runny-nosed children grabbed at me, and I couldn't shake them loose. My cameras fell off my shoulders, and I had to shout for help. Some adults pushed them back until I was able to reach the street and get into our waiting car. It took us past the outdoor market square to visit the Mentsekun Hospital of Tibetan Medicine.

The hospital treats six hundred to seven hundred outpatients a day and has twenty beds. It was originally created by the Thirteenth Dalai Lama in 1915, and it was modernized in the 1960's. Now it combines modern medicine with ancient Tibetan medicine.

Tibetan medicine has a long history. As early as the eighth century a famed physician summed up the experience of Tibetan folk doctors in a "Code of Medicine," consisting of thirty volumes which laid a solid foundation for Tibetan medicine. Further systemization of the code was catalogued in the seventeenth century in a book called "Blue Glaze." It was illustrated with seventy-nine colored charts of herb specimens collected from various parts of Tibet in 1704. We saw the original charts hanging on the walls of a hospital room where an elderly Tibetan doctor with a white, whispy beard was examining patients. His name, Dr. Pencog, was a common one among traditional Tibetan herbal doctors.

The Tibetan custom of dissecting dead bodies had a beneficial side effect, for it enabled doctors to gain an early knowledge of anatomy and physiology in ancient times. The ancient charts show that they also had a scientific knowledge of the nervous and circulatory systems and the development of the human embryo. Amazingly, in the middle ages, they already had a scientific conception of the origin and evolution of man, which is shown in charts depicting the different stages of evolution from fish (aquatics) to the tortoise (reptiles) to the pig (mammals).

After examining the pulse of his patient, who was suffering from a stomach pain, Dr. Pencog asked a few questions and prescribed some medicinal herbs to be picked up in pill form at the hospital pharmacy. Prescriptions may involve from one to a

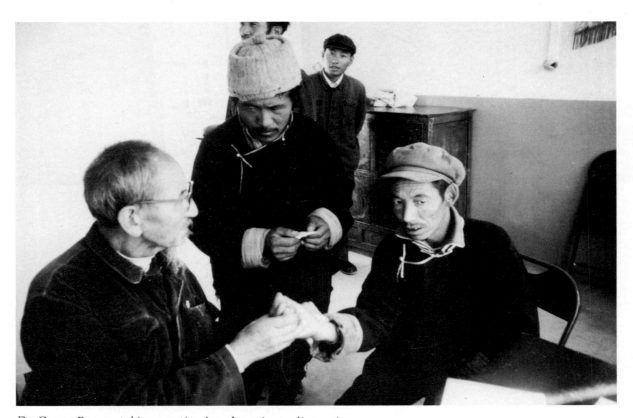

Dr. Gunga Pencog taking a patient's pulse prior to diagnosis.

Tibetan doctors, using Tibetan calendar and astronomical charts, forecast the most propitious time to plant crops.

hundred ingredients. Medicines are also prepared from animal parts and minerals. Some remedies in the past were based on the theory that a strange connection existed between certain animal substances, parts of the human body and some illnesses. If, for example, the eye diseases were treated by an extract from the gall of an ox, leprosy was treated with dog's liver. The tongue of a dog was believed to heal flesh wounds.

Although those analogies may sound ab-surd, they are like other ancient cures being restudied today to discover if there was, in fact, some basis for them. Some Tibetan herbs grow at an altitude of over twelve thousand feet. In 1840 Dr. Dema Pencog authored a "Compendium of Medicinal Herbs" that listed fourteen hundred different kinds of medicine and gave a detailed explanation as to the nature and use of each one.

Dr. Minmayihsi and other senior officials of the hospital received us with cups of green tea in a reception room whose cushioned divans were covered with multicolored rugs and the floors with embossed green Tibetan carpets.

Most patients we saw were Tibetans in their teens and older, but ethnic Chinese also use the hospital, especially when troubled by rheumatism, which is easily contracted in the Lhasa altitude. Judging by the long lines of patients who get prescriptions filled free at three pharmacy counters in the lobby, many Tibetans rely on their traditional medicine.

The Chinese were impressed by the curative qualities of Tibetan herbal medicine, but they also introduced modern diagnostic equipment so that patients can have their blood pressure taken, get cardiographic readings and also receive blood and other laboratory tests. Vaccination and Chinese acupuncture also are available. Of the 127 doctors on the staff, all but one, a Chinese cardiologist, are traditional Tibetan doctors. Thirty-seven are women.

Dr. Minmayihsi said that records were kept on each patient, but that the data and the work of the hospital had not been surveyed by Western researchers. The superstitious practices often associated with Tibetan medicine have been eliminated, he maintained.

About three hundred varieties of Tibetan medicine are dispensed, often with instructions that two or three pills should be taken three times a day. Tibetan children, who frequently suffer fever and pneumonia, balk at taking the round pills, many of which look like large roasted coffee beans. They are sent to other hospitals for antibiotics.

The Tibetan medicines, which the hospital officials say are more effective than Chinese herbs, are exported to virtually all provinces of China. The hospital manages high-altitude farms on which the exotic herbs are grown. In the treatment of rheumatism, the afflicted parts of the body are washed with a solution of herbal medicine, and then pills are prescribed.

Because of their diet, poor sanitary conditions and irregular eating habits (the Tibetans eat whenever they are hungry), stomach ulcers are common. Tibetan herdsmen eat mutton and yak-meat that at times is virtually raw and live on a staple diet of tsampa.

Dr. Minmayihsi, whose research department is carrying out studies into the cause of disease in Tibet and into preventive medicine, began learning his art from his father, who was also a traditional doctor. At the age of eighteen, Dr. Minmayihsi was sent to a Buddhist temple to become a Lama, and then was sent to Mentsekun, where he studied herbal medicine, grammar, astronomy and what he refers to as superstitions to mislead the people.

Like other aspects of society under the Theocracy, medicine was tinged with superstition and brought little help to the ordinary Tibetan. A warning in the "Code of Medicine" read, "No doctor shall treat any disease, even if curable, contracted by the poor, the unbelievers or life-extinguishers (butchers)."

Many sicknesses were considered to be the result of sin, and the victim was turned over to the exorcist instead of a doctor. Often monks were called in to murmur apt, sacred texts; the mere recantation of them was believed to have positive magi-

Dispensing pills made from herbs.

cal powers, even if it was not understood. Another method was to buy a goat that was about to be slaughtered and tie a red ribbon about his neck. As long as the ribbon lasted the animal could not then be slaughtered, and this delay was believed to save the life of the sick person. Today the "Code of Medicine" is being restudied by Tibetan and Han scientists and incorporated into modern medicine in keeping with the current slogan "Let the past serve the present."

Leaving the hospital we honked our way through the curious pedestrians and winding streets towards new Lhasa, which is quite a different type of city. It was built during the 1960's on the open spaces around the foot of Red Hill and stretches about a mile west of the Potala. The streets

Medical thankas show amazingly accurate anatomical charts from the fifteenth century and illustrations of over one thousand medicinal herbs painted in 1704.

A street in new Lhasa.

are broad, straight and tree-lined. Almost half of the 120,000 Han Chinese in Tibet live in new Lhasa in gray brick apartments built around courtyards. Along the main road named Yanhe are shops, small factories, schools, tea houses, a post office, an auditorium and government administrative buildings which are distinguished by their metal roofs.

In the old society, Yanhe road was known as "the street of beggars," for it was here that over half of Lhasa's several thousand beggars lived in misery, rotting alive in a foul slum, overrun with wild scavanger dogs. It was also the home of shackled thieves, some mutilated or blinded for attempting to survive by stealing. Here the hopeless and starving came to die and the mad came to feel at home.

No report of Lhasa under the Theocracy was complete without a mention of filth, dogs or glut of beggars. Theos Bernard wrote about "the streets of Lhasa resembling streams of sewage and human filth .. One of the first things to jolt me was the use of the streets for toilets."

Of beggars he noted —

"... the lot of the beggars at best is far from an enviable one, to judge from the ones you see, with scarce a real flicker of life among them ...

The sight of new construction is prevalent in Lhasa.

117

"We joined a rapidly increasing crowd, attracted to the sight of a human being taking his last breaths while prostrated on the kerb, with almost the entire calf of one leg eaten off and the heel of the other foot gone; and there was all the gore that colors such a scene. It appears that one of the dogs had become a little hungry and helped himself, and the fellow was not the recipient of gathering sympathies and of unheard of aid."

In 1949 Lowell Thomas, Jr., who visited Tibet with his father on the invitation of the Dalai Lama, wrote of old Lhasa:

"Nothing is known of modern plumbing. Refuse piles up in all corners . . . once a year these offal heaps are transferred to the fields to stimulate crops. The odors are not entirely pleasant. The nobles hold scented handkerchiefs to their noses as they ride along . . . dead animals are tossed in refuse piles to be fought over and devoured by the city's scavangers — thousands of mangy dogs and ravens."

When the Buddhist theocracy was forced out, the people learned to take fate into their own hands. The PLA rounded up the sick and wild dogs and put them out of their misery. Shovels and brooms were distributed, and the people were enlisted in a clean up campaign that lasted months. People were forced to wash themselves and their clothing and to build toilets, even if they were primitive, in secluded places. Electricity was made available to everyone, and cold running water was installed in every courtyard. Neighborhood committees were set up to supervise and encourage citizen cooperation.

Although the streets are now clean and living standards have been raised for the ordinary Tibetans, Lhasa still has not been able to completely eliminate beggary and poverty.

The next day we met with four influential Tibetan officials and discussed the problem.

"We have seen some very poor people on the streets here," said Top. "We can see that conditions are not as good as the rest of China. Why?"

We were talking to a former Lama who served as Secretary General to the Fourteenth Dalai Lama, to a noble Kaloon (a high administrative official) in the old Tibetan government and to two Living Buddhas. All were now members of the Political Consultative Congress. The Kaloon official, Lhalu Tsewong-Dorje, who was formerly Minister of Food, stabbed a finger into the arm of the stuffed chair and looked troubled. He wore fine Tibetan clothes and had a sophisticated appearance.

"Yes, you can see a few poor people. That is why the key problem is to raise agricultural production. Each person earns according to their ability and, according to this principle, we can't practise egalitarianism. If a person works hard, he can be richer. I can say that in Tibet no one is starving now and everyone has some clothing and shelter. The standard is much higher than when people were slaves. I can tell you that from personal observation. Twenty years ago the streets were full of beggars."

One of the Living Buddhas who came to talk with us was a woman, a former nun named Doujebamo. She was an attractive woman who wore her long hair pulled back except for a fringe of bangs across her high forehead. She had pleasing, even features and a madonna smile. A green Chinese jacket almost covered her pink silk blouse worn with a black Tibetan tunic and a traditional apron. A yellow scarf, the color of purity, was draped loosely around her neck. She had been discovered at the age of four and brought to the Sangding Temple in Loka. She rubbed her delicate hands together and spoke softly in Tibetan.

"I was eighteen when the Dalai Lama left in 1959, some of his armed supporters took me along forcibly. The band rode until their horses died under them," she said. Then, after a two-month journey, they walked through a mountain pass into India.

Han Chinese in Lhasa's People's Park.

*Former nun, Doujebamo, once a
living Buddha is now a member
of the Consultative Congress.*

*Former Secretary General to the
Fourteenth Dalai Lama is politically
active in the new government.*

Four months later she escaped with a small group and came back home where she renounced her priestly role, married and became a delegate to the National People's Congress in Peking. Now, at thirty-eight years of age, she is politically active and deeply concerned about the future of Tibet.

She was accompanied by another Living Buddha, Shengqing Loshangrancun, a vigorous and handsome man of forty who was a vice chairman of the Tibetan People's Congress. He looked splendid in his dark robe of the finest wool, sashed with a slash of bright purple and topped with a wide brimmed hat. He had not taken part in the revolt as had the former Secretary General, Tudeng Danda, who said he once had blind faith in the Dalai Lama's government and was active in preparing the resistance.

"Why didn't you flee with the Dalai Lama?"

"Because he didn't tell me he was going. When I woke up they were gone. Now I am glad I stayed even though I was arrested and imprisoned for three years. I came to remold my outlook."

We learned that the main concern of these former religious leaders was no longer acquiring merits for the next reincarnation but was with life here and now. "Raising productivity is the most important task facing the Tibetan people today," said the former nun.

Mr. Shengquing agreed. "I think the biggest problem is how to implement modernization and the construction of a new Tibet. We must solve the problems of agriculture, animal husbandry, transport and communications. We must think of future generations."

An ancient pillar is inscribed with a treaty between Lhasa and Peking.

5. The Wrath Of The Serfs

The younger generation in Tibet, as in every other country, is more interested in the future than the past. But lest they forget the bitter past and the hardships their ancestors endured for centuries, the school children are taken in groups to the "Museum of Revolution" in Lhasa to see a frankly propagandistic narrative display of clay sculptures entitled *The Wrath of the Serfs*.

We were not particularly eager to go, but went out of deference to our hosts who had arranged, much to my disappointment, to keep the school children out so they would not distract us. We were met by a young, aesthetic looking Tibetan in a gray wool robe revealing one shoulder and arm in a green sweater. Pushing aside a black curtain he led us into a dimly lit hall where 106 life-size, starkly realistic clay figures had been arranged in a series of vividly melodramatic scenes showing "the evil world of old Tibet."

The sculptures were made of natural rich brown clay modeled on wooden armatures with careful attention to detail. The figures conveyed intense feeling. Accurate musculature and veining exuded tension, while the faces and idealized bodies expressed fear, despair, pain, humiliation, rage and, finally, hope and determination. Large inset glass eyes accentuated the emotionalism. Garments were realistically rendered, down to patches and stitches. Real objects or "props," such as guns, chains, whips, ropes, wooden canques and even an umbrella, were intermittently incorporated with sculpted facsimilies to heighten the immediacy of affect.

The tableaux were arranged against painted or bas-relief backgrounds of realistic scenery and buildings. A tape-recorded commentary explained each scene while music played softly. To me, the overall impression was one of almost childish terror equivalent to what I had experienced on a tour through the horror chambers of Madam Tussaud's wax museum in London. As in Madam Tussaud's, all the tableaux were based on ac-

tual people and incidents but they conveyed an exaggerated affect.

The Wrath of the Serfs is the work of several Han and Tibetan art teachers who traveled five thousand kilometers around Tibet interviewing former serfs about their own experiences in order to create scenes typical of serfdom. The entire project took a year and a half to finish. It consists of four sections. Three concern the life of the serfs under the rule of the three estate holders — the nobility, the monasteries and the "kasha" or local government. The last section shows the "liberation."

The first scene consists of a series of tableaux entitled "The Manor of Crimes." It has an archetypal dramatic beginning — the arrival and assembly of characters. A line of serfs trudge up a mountain under a dark, ominous sky in a snow storm. The theme of misery is painfully communicated as they stagger under heavy sacks of yak-butter, chingko barley and rice which they are transporting to the manor house. One serf carries the silk-robed landowner "piggy back," according to the old custom, while an armed overseer shelters the rich man with an umbrella, symbol of high status. Not far ahead an emaciated old man has collapsed under his load while his anguished daughter and little granddaughter, clad in fluttering rags, grieve over him. An overseer raises his whip but is stopped by a young serf. Meanwhile, back at the manor, two of the landlord's lackeys take a donkey and boy from a blind man who couldn't pay his rent. In the stable a woman serf grinds barley while her starving child cries pitiably.

The scenes got even more dramatic as we entered the next section called "Reactionary Religious Authority," where the theme of oppression and conflict is reiterated with added impact. A monk is pushing a screaming boy into a box to be buried alive in the foundation of a new monastery chapel called the "Hall of Sacrifice." Behind the struggling child stands a Living Buddha and a fierce guardian Lama holding his thunderbolt staff. The ago-

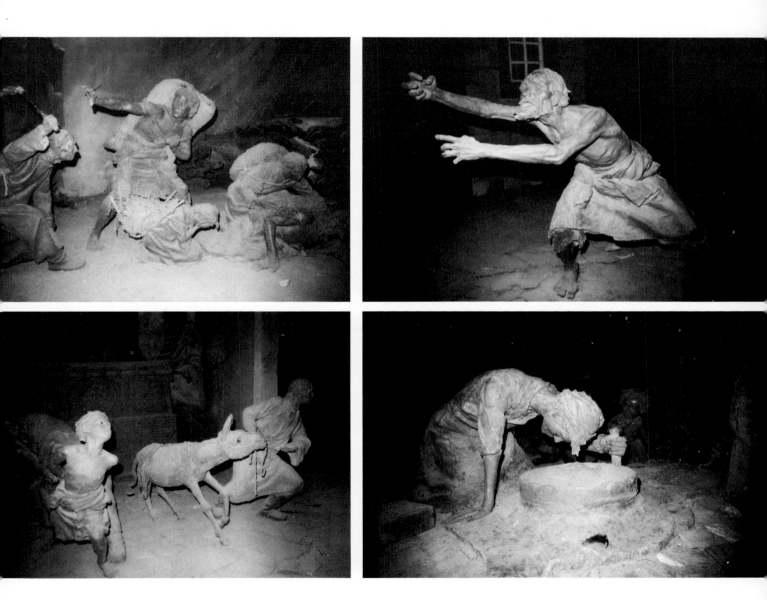

126

the kasha, but each time they struck terror into the hearts of the serf-owners."

The last scene shows the worst punishment of all — exile. A serf, lying face down, back to front on an ox, is being sent to a wild, uninhabitable mountain area to die slowly without the guidance of a monk to save him from the eighteen hells. The tortured serf has spikes under his fingernails and a wooden canque around his neck. His wretched daughter follows with a look of such touching pathos in her black eyes that I could only gasp in horror.

By the time we reached the last section, "Struggle and Hope," I felt like a nervous wreck. However, the mood changed from total oppression to open revolt. The serfs

nized parents protest in vain. The Museum guide calmly informed us that this was a common practise in Tibet (as it was in China and Europe in the Middle Ages), and was done in remote areas until the democratic reforms. He later showed us photos of two boys whom he claimed had been rescued in 1957 before they were to be buried alive in the foundation of a monastery being renovated in Gyatso County.

The third section, "The Barbarous Kasha," depicts officials of the local government dispensing their feudal justice, and consists of a group of sub-scenes of escalating brutality that reveal the extremes of the misuse of power: imprisonment, torture and murder with variations on the theme of family disruption. One beaten serf is being dragged in chains to the dungeons. Another woman, tied to the punishment stake in front of the Potala, is about to have her heart gouged out. "Her name was Hor Lhamo," said the Museum guide, "and she was killed in exactly this way in 1918 for leading a revolt against the county government. In the half century before liberation," he went on, "the serfs rose up in more than a hundred large scale revolts. They were cruelly put down by

127

rise up, kill the guards and open the prisons. They are shown lifting a baby from the dungeon below the Potala. "The youngest prisoner was a two-day-old girl born in the dungeon."

The narrative ends at this turning point. The young and strong, in quasi-military garb, bearing weapons, join the Liberation Army in the mountains, where together they stand victorious in a last dramatic tableau reminiscent of a classical stance in old Chinese opera. The impact of this highly theatrical narrative realism was physical as well as mental. I felt shaken and exhausted by the time we left the dim hall into a brightly lit exhibit of present day life. From a propagandistic point of view, as well as for artistic effect, *The Wrath of the Serfs* is an undeniable success.

6. Visit To A Peasant's Commune

One sunny afternoon we were taken to visit the Guangming Commune which lies on a brown, stony, northern slope in Lhasa Valley. Here some peasant families worked together on a relatively prosperous commune composed of five production teams engaged in farming and animal husbandry.

The walls of their white adobe houses were studded with cakes of drying yak dung, and red flags flew over the gates in place of the traditional prayer flags. We were met in a spacious, flower-decked courtyard by the Chairman, who welcomed us to the commune. Like most of the other members he had been a serf before the land reforms in the 1960's, and therefore had just one name, Nouchi. He was a thin, fragile man with only one eye and skin as wrinkled and parched as the dry earth in the fields. All around us we could see the effects of a drought, and poor harvests were expected for the season, but Nouchi was sanguine about the failure.

He invited us into a low house with red ceiling beams where a group of weather-beaten men in their work clothes waited to brief us about conditions on the commune. A smiling man in a spotted apron and soot-smeared face and hands poured us greasy yak-butter tea that tasted like smoke.

It was the first time Nouchi had given a briefing to foreign visitors, and he was understandably nervous. He was illiterate and could not read the details from notes, but his partners prompted him as he slowly told us about the commune.

"The commune," he said, "consists of 372 families with a population of 1,627 people. We formed the commune in 1972, and we work the land with some yaks, 5 small tractors and 11 larger ones. The grain

Yaks plowing.

Men help care for their children.

*Yak-dung cakes drying on the wall
are used for fuel.*

*Flowering vines shade the veranda
of a commune home.*

production teams distributed three tenths of a ton of grain per person last year, which means we had good meals and

134

enough left over to sell or trade in the free market for meat, clothing and household items. We also have a reserve in case of poor harvests, and, if necessary, we can get a loan from the State, but this has not yet been necessary."

He explained that in the past the land was divided between the big landowners or "chhuda" (consisting of the monasteries and nobles) and the small landowners, "mamchung," who were obliged to serve the "chhuda" by providing at least one man per family to work on the overlord's land in exchange for such food as the estate owner saw fit to feed him. Other members of the "mamchung's" family could also be called into service when needed. Seed, plows and money for marriages, religious ceremonies and funerals were borrowed from the estate owners at an uncontrolled rate of interest. When debts could not be repaid, which eventually was almost always the case, the small landowner was obliged to become a serf or indentured laborer. He was bound to the service of the big landowner who then took three-fourths of everything the serf produced on his own land.

Once the small landowner had become a serf it lasted, not only for life, but for generations, since the children were held responsible for the hopeless debts that had accumulated. The estate owner had complete control over this feudal relationship. He had the right to lend or sell members of the serf's family. Serfs could not wear the same colors, sit in the same seats, eat the same food or even use the same vocabulary. Serfs were forbidden to learn, so they eventually became what Nouchi referred to as "little more than talking animals." To raise their eyes above the knees of their betters was a crime. The estate owner had the right to dispense justice as he pleased. There was no central code of conduct or civil law governing the treatment of peasants. Floggings and barbaric punishments such as hamstringing were common and

Chambayuka and her three-year-old son.

the tenants had no right of appeal.

There were also some benevolent estate owners and some absentee owners who were not aware of the cruelties committed by their overseers. The whole system, however, was open to constant and sadistic exploitation, and this was recognized by the Fourteenth Dalai Lama who, in the 1950's, attempted some reforms in education as well as land ownership. His plans were blocked by the powerful landlords and big monasteries who feared, rightly, that any reforms would weaken their positions and topple the whole system.

Formerly every town and remote village had its own monastery filled with monks to administer to the everyday needs of the people. The presence of the monks was

Chambayuka and her family live with her mother.

necessary on all occasions except during childbirth, when the woman was left alone and unattended. It was the custom in the countryside to give birth in the stables. If something went wrong, as it often did because of the unsanitary conditions, a Lama or exorcist would be called in to offer prayers or talismans, but any help from a medical doctor or midwife was inconceivable. Only in the homes of the landowners would a woman stay in bed while others cared for her and the child.

Because of superstitions and medical ignorance, the infant mortality rate was enormously high, with over one half of the

Portrait of Mao Zedong hangs in a peasant's home.

children dying at birth. Those that survived often succumbed in the first years to the cold or infection. Babies were seldom washed, and only then in cold water or water that had been warmed slightly in the mother's mouth before spraying it over the infant. However, unlike old China where unwanted infant girls were often thrown into pits or death towers to die, the Tibetans never practised female infanticide, although boys were favored during the primitive infant care and general upbringing.

Free medical care is now provided in the Guangming Commune by four "barefoot doctors," each with six months training, who also attend at childbirth. There is

Women do most of the field work.

also a Tibetan doctor, trained in Western as well as traditional herbal medicine, who runs a clinic in the main compound beside the primary school. For more serious illnesses patients are sent to Lhasa hospital.

After the briefing we visited an elderly widow with seven grown children. She lived with her daughter and son-in-law and three grandchildren in a typical two-storied house built around an inner courtyard facing south to trap all available sunlight. The family owned two pigs, three cows, six chickens and three sheep. The animals were kept in shelters within a surrounding wall near the gate. The kitchen was downstairs beside a storeroom filled with hay and wood. Dung cakes to be used as fuel were piled high near the front steps. The front veranda was shaded by blooming vines and flowers. We ascended the wooden stairway into the central room which was wallpapered with newspapers. The family was a "Five Insured Family,"

which meant they had been guaranteed food, clothing, shelter, medical care and burial ceremonies by the commune.

The old mother received us and introduced us to her daughter, Chambayuka, a sturdy, full-cheeked woman of thirty, who was wearing a flowered kerchief around her head and a long black robe under the

Woman harvesting.

137

typical apron. She carried a fat three-year-old boy on her hip who sucked milk from her breasts whenever he felt the urge. We sat and talked in a small room with three beds, a table and some beautifully lacquered chests that looked as if they would have been more appropriate in a manor house. Chambayuka had three children whom the grandmother cared for while her daughter worked in the fields. Chambayuka, like the other women in the commune, rose at 6 A.M., went to bed at 10 P.M. and worked eleven days before she got one day off. At harvest time, there are no days off. Her husband, who works in a factory in Lhasa, returns home one day a week.

In the past the custom of women taking more than one husband by marrying all the brothers in one family was practised in almost half of the rural marriages. This was done in spite of the surplus of single women (resulting from the fact that a quarter of the men had entered monasteries). Polyandry was meant to keep the family and property together and avoid feuds, but it was clearly a most arduous life for the wife who was obliged to work in the fields as well as serve all her husbands and bear the children who, no matter who their fathers were, belonged to the eldest brother.

In the cities, however, polygamy, allowing men to have a number of wives, was practised. If a woman was found guilty of committing adultery, the husband had the right to cut off the tip of her nose and paint it black so she must wear the ugly scar forever. Wife murder was not uncommon and was punishable by a fine or blood money.

Chambayuka counted herself as fortunate, not only because women have achieved an almost equal status, but also because her family and commune were among the well off. She shopped in the commune store, which stocks the same basic necessities and small luxuries as the department store in Lhasa. The State subsidizes necessities to offset the high cost of transportation to Tibet. It loses money on

such items as tea and chemical fertilizer and makes a profit on cigarettes and alcoholic beverages.

Chambayuka had more money than the average peasant because in 1978 the per capita cash income in the commune was 257 yuan or about $140. The commune, once it has deducted a grain allocation for each member and put some in reserve, sells its surplus grain to the State. If the quota is exceeded there is a 50 per cent bonus. The commune in 1978 produced 7,500 tons of grain and paid an agricultural tax of 13.1 tons.

Chambayuka told us that the women tend the animals, gather dung and wood for fuel and churn milk into butter for tsampa, the mulch-like mixture of powdered roast barley and yak-butter tea with salt which they eat with their fingers. They also do most of the field work while the men "go out on assignment."

"What kind?" I asked.

"They drive carts, some do sidelines as stone smiths, everyone has a quota. If we exceed it, we get a bonus, so we work hard to get more money."

The men also did the plowing with tractors and teams of powerful yaks. We could see them in the surrounding fields. Red wool tassels flopped over the animal's foreheads to frighten away any evil spirits that might still be hanging about.

For centuries yaks were the backbone of the Tibetan economy. Besides being the main beast of burden and, until trucks were introduced, the main means of transport, they supply food, shelter and clothing. Their hair is spun into a variety of materials used for tents, covers and clothing. Yak hides are put to a diversity of uses including coats, boots, laces and even circular boats, called coracles. In the rural areas, babies are carried in yak-hide bags and sleep under yak-wool blankets on soft, little beds of yak-dung ashes.

Yaks are as old as Tibet. The ancient Tibetans domesticated wild yaks, although some breeds still live in the wild state. Yaks are as big as North American bisons,

but it is remarkable that they can grow so large and strong on the coarse grass and thistles they are obliged to forage with their thick tongues. The Tibetans claim that it is their large hearts that enable them to labor at high altitudes while other draft animals that the Chinese have been experimentally introducing into Tibet weary quickly. However, when compared to the output of work animals at lower altitudes, the yak cannot labor for nearly as long.

Yak-butter and meat are staple foods. The animals are usually killed by suffocation to keep the blood in the meat. Most of the slaughtering is done in the fall by Muslims, as Buddhists are forbidden to take life. They can, however, eat meat if killed by someone else. Then the meat is cut up, wrapped in hide and put in boxes made of dung and left to freeze until spring. In the old society these boxes of meat were often brought as offerings to the monasteries where the monks, robed in crimson-dyed yak-wool and yellow hide boots, washed down the yak meat with yak-butter tea while seated on yak-wool carpets around yak-leather chests.

The horns and bones of the yak are carved into all kinds of ornaments for temples and homes, which are protected by yak-dung cakes piled into walls to ward off the murderous winter wind. Country boys carry yak-hair sling shots and yak-hide flint bags containing a cotton-like substance which is held on top of a stone while it is struck with the flint to make fire. When lit it is set on a pile of dried yak dung which is still the main fuel in Tibet. The Chinese have tried in vain to persuade the Tibetans to use coal for fuel so the yak dung can be used as much needed fertilizer. The Tibetans, however, have stubbornly refused, claiming they can't stand the smell of coal.

Neither Chambayuka or her mother had learned to read because there had never been any schools for ordinary children in Tibet. There had been two lay schools in old Lhasa that served about three hundred children from the ruling class, and there was religious education for those who joined the monasteries. But most Tibetans over thirty years old in the commune were still illiterate.

The rationale for this policy of denying education to anyone except the monks was explained in a book written in 1968 by Thubten Jigme Norbu, the brother of the present Dalai Lama.

. . . "It has always been and still is our belief that there is no higher goal than religious enlightenment. A secular education corresponds only to secular needs, and in Tibet these are minimal. The son of a nomad knows all there is to know about the life before him by the time he is nine or ten years old. So with the son or daughter of a farmer . . . Reading and writing are virtually unnecessary for there is no such thing as secular literature in Tibet, and one of the values of having such a large body of monks is that in every village in every part of the country there are monks readily available to read the scriptures or recite them, to the villagers, often adding a sermon or moral instruction to the reading and performing a rite and offering prayers, benefits that no layman could get by a mere reading of the scriptures on his own . . . Monks also are always available to perform death and commemorative rites and to fulfill any other ritual needs a family might have . . .

"What intellectual development any layman wants he wants in terms of his knowledge and understanding of the scriptures, and this is always open to him. Further knowledge, to anyone with so clear a sense of direction, is meaningless."

The concept that no layman would even want to know anything more than the scriptures, and that farmers and nomads were naturally inferior, was commonly accepted by the monkhood. Knowledge was jealously guarded. The idea of sending a peasant child to lay school was obviously as inconceivable as sending a yak to college. When the Communists introduced public education in the 1950's, it incurred

Hauling hewn rock for new construction.

the hostility of the monasteries who had hitherto monopolized learning and also the wrath of the nobility because of the way schools were set up to give privileges to the children of serfs. For the State encouraged peasant parents to send their children to school by subsidizing them. Schools not only provided teaching and all school supplies, but food and clothing for the whole family as well.

The Guangming Commune has a primary and a secondary school. And we were told that in 1979 70 to 75 per cent of all Tibetan children attended school. Over 6,000 free primary schools have been established since 1959, most of them in the past 10 years. In 1979 there were altogether 50 secondary and 22 vocational schools, 4 universities and 2 teacher's institutes, with a total of about 260,000 students in all of Tibet. About 800 additional students are in medical schools in other parts of China and over 1,000 Tibetan students are in Institutes for National Minorities.

Educational reform is having an enlightening effect on Tibet. Yet twenty years later we could still see the scars that had been carved into the minds and bodies of the peasants and former serfs in Guangming Commune by centuries of enforced ignorance and humiliation. Some, like Nouchi, the one-eyed leader, wore the marks of cruel physical punishments, while others still looked mentally bewildered and shocked. Some could not seem to shake the demeaning old customs, such as walking with their heads bent low or sticking out their tongues in greeting as they were required to do when they saw their masters, as a sign of respect and acknowledgement of their own inferiority.

The difference between the stunted older generations and the bright, educated younger generation is both sad and encouraging. As we were leaving the farm house, the tough, illiterate grandmother tugged at my sleeve. I looked at her and saw how time and hardship had chiseled furrows of sorrow upon her face. She held up a picture of her youngest son and told us he had just graduated from medical school. Her smile of happy pride and joy told me more about the changes in Tibet than statistics could possibly convey.

141

Votive lamps burn constantly in the Jokhang.

7. The Jokhang: Temple Of The Precious One

Gold gilt prayer wheel embossed with Buddhist scriptures on the roof of the Jokhang Temple.

Willow tree in front of the Jokhang Temple was planted by Princess Wen Cheng in 652 A.D.

The smallpox pillar was pitted by superstitious people gouging out the inscription to make medicine.

In the heart of old Lhasa, tucked in amongst the white stone, flat-roofed houses, stands the Jokhang Temple, meaning "Temple of the Precious One." It is the Holy of Holies and is revered as the most spiritual center of Tibet.

The Temple was only a ten-minute walk from our guest house, so we strolled down the wide, tree-lined street which led from the new city to the narrow, circular streets of old Lhasa. When the people spotted us, they dropped whatever they were doing to stare and smile. Then, because there always seems to be plenty of time and curiosity in Tibet, most of them followed along, while the children actually ran around us in circles, squealing with glee and grabbing our hands. After all, it was not every day that strangers from a far-off land came to visit Lhasa.

The Jokhang Temple itself is enclosed by an iron fence and a gate facing onto a narrow cobblestone street. When we arrived, crowds of people were milling around. Some had come just to watch us, while others were fingering prayer beads. Still others prostrated themselves on the ground before the Temple gate. Nearby stood the old "treaty edict pillar," inscribed in both Chinese characters and Tibetan script, which records an alliance concluded in 821 A.D. between a Tibetan King and a Tang dynasty Emperor, Mu Yuang. It read: "Uncle (Chinese Emperor) and nephew (The King) have agreed that their governments are like one, forming an alliance of grand peace . . . We will respect forever the good relations . . ."

Directly across from the Temple stood another stone tablet, erected by the Chinese in 1794, that bore the inscribed procedure to be adopted in case of an outbreak of smallpox. The children in the street scrambled up on the tablet to get a better look at the blue-eyed, light-haired foreigner. Ironically the face of smallpox pillar was as pockmarked as a victim of the disease because many of the people, believing the stone itself had curative powers, had for decades scooped out bits of it to make into powder for medicine. Just behind the pitted tablet stood a forlorn weeping willow tree, said to have been planted by Princess Wen Cheng, the Chinese wife of the first Tibetan King, Songtsen Gampo. The tree is now dry and twisted, which is not surprising if it really was, as claimed, planted in 652 A.D.

The Temple is reputed to have been erected in the same year to enshrine a statue of the sacred Sakyamuni Buddha (in Tibetan, Jawa Rinpoche) allegedly brought to Tibet by the Princess when she came to marry the King. It also houses images brought by his Nepalese wife. The legends surrounding the building of the Temple are many and varied but most agree that the Temple was built over an underground lake.

It was not long before the streets around the Temple were so jammed with inquisitive citizens that not even the government

Guardian lion watches over the temple courtyard.

officials, who travelled in Chinese made cars with curtained windows, could get through. A frantic policeman in a white uniform scowled as he tried to clear the streets, but the people were too busy being friendly and posing for pictures. They ignored him. We decided it was time to disappear into the Holy of Holies.

Two lama monks with beatific smiles,

Doorway to the main Chapel.

big ears, and holding palms together greeted us in the carmine-pillared courtyard. Like ladies in formal attire, they hitched up their crimson robes above their yak-hide boots to avoid tripping as they led us through a massive red wooden door embellished with golden knockers. A "No Photo" sign hung over it. This led through a short passage, protected on both sides by an array of hideous guardian figures, to another door which opened into an inner courtyard. Suddenly, all was enchantment. Above a pillared veranda was a dazzle of golden rooftops, dripping with tinkling brass bells and frosted with dragons, lions, mythical birds and beasts. They cavorted

The chief monks of the Jokhang Temple with a member of the Department of Cultural Relics.

Inner courtyard in the Temple of the Precious One.

147

A lama carries a yak-butter torch to light our way through the temple.

over the eaves sticking out their golden tongues.

Directly opposite the courtyard was an outer chapel with altars filled with offerings of coins, incense and other gifts presented by worshippers. To the left was the throne where the Dalai Lama used to sit to watch religious ceremonies. In another dark passage on the right was a small shrine dedicated to the Water-Dragon, or spirit of the lake on which the Temple was built. Legend relates that Princess Wen Cheng, who was an expert in astrological divination, pronounced the lake as the most auspicious place to build a temple. She said: "Tibet is like a she-demon on her back; her heart is at the lake before the Potala, and if a temple is built on it, the Dharma will prevail in Tibet."

The legend continues that the Nepalese wife suspected trickery so the King threw his ring in the air claiming that he would build the temple where it fell. It fell in the middle of the lake and struck a rock upon which a stupa sprang up, and this was considered a lucky sign. The lake was filled with stones and the best craftsmen from Tibet as well as China and Nepal were called to build the temple that is known today as the Jokhang or Lhasa Tsuglakhang. The chief Lama showed us a large, loose stone that supposedly keeps the springs feeding the lake from bubbling up and engulfing Lhasa. To prevent such a disaster, offerings were thrown down to the Dragon once a year. He related this terrifying information with a sweet smile and a twinkle, but I thought I could hear some ominous rumblings below us.

We came into the central hall of the

Deities and Guardians of the Four Directions preside in smaller shrines.

main temple. On both sides of the entrance were frescoes showing Princess Wen Cheng's journey to Lhasa in a horse carriage, the building of the temple and various religious ceremonies. In the middle of the hall sat a colossal, gilded image of the Future Buddha draped in rich yellow brocade. It reached to the open skylight on the second story. The Buddha's hands were raised in benediction, and it was protected by a halo of carved monsters. Two more Buddhas of equal splendor, representing the Buddhas of the Past and Present, flanked it. A particularly delicate one of Buddha Chenresik, with eleven faces and four pairs of arms, expressing his all-seeing, all-embracing compassion stood nearby. Golden chalices held burning wicks on the altar tables before each image. We stood in awe, and when I told him of my appreciation for these marvels, the chief monk broke his expression of modest pride with a beam of unconcealed joy.

"These are only a few of our treasures," he said in a whispery voice. "Come, you will see." He was a gentle, shaven-headed man, about sixty, and he shuffled ahead carrying a yak-butter torch to light our way. The odor of the rancid, burning butter assaulted our nostrils as he led us to the left through a dark, circular passageway, which ran around the outside of the central court of the temple.

Chapels were placed around the main hall like boxes in a theater, separated by brightly painted pillars. We advanced from shrine to shrine, each decked with hosts of golden, silk-robed images, silently bestowing messages from other lives in unreal worlds where illusion and reality began to blur.

One Goddess was particularly memorable, both because of her exquisite, pale beauty and also because she was completely modeled out of "sacred clay," which had become so by being sprinkled with water in which a Dalai Lama had washed his hands. We finally arrived at the main attraction, the Sakyamuni Bud-

dha, the oldest and most precious statue in Tibet, allegedly brought from China thirteen centuries earlier by Princess Wen Cheng. Since then, it has been gilded and regilded with gold leaf and encrusted with jewels. The holy image was guarded by fearsome monsters and hidden behind a heavy iron mesh curtain.

Another monk, named Gyatso, who, among other jobs in the temple, took care of the Buddha, unlocked the huge padlock and strained his arms to pull back the chains. Gyatso had oiled his thin, twisted mustache with yak-butter which gave him a unique fragrance and an uncanny resemblance to Salvador Dali. He gave us a cavalier smile as we stepped inside the shrine to behold the most sacred splendor of all.

The statue presides serenely on a silver throne, behind an altar table laden with flaming chalices of gold and silver. The tableau is flanked by silver dragons twisting up golden pillars, surrounded by a galaxy of disciples, and protected by the usual horde of fierce guardians. On the Buddha's head is a golden crown in the

Lama Gyatso oils his moustache with yak-butter.

150

Buddha of the Future.

Buddha of the Past.

Chenresik, Buddha of Compasion, in his all-seeing all-embracing aspect, symbolized by many heads and arms.

The fierce aspect of the Buddha of Compassion; Buddhas often have many aspects.

king sported a dapper mustache exactly like our monk, Gyatso — or was it the other way around?

From 652 to 1660 the temple had been enlarged eight times. Rich decoration was added in the fifteenth century by Tsongkhapa, the founder of the Yellow Hat sect, and again by the Great Fifth. The four-storied temple now contains 20 prayer halls and over 300 statues. Between 1972 and 1975 the government allotted 700,000

The temple's most sacred and oldest Buddha, Sakyamuni, is protected by a padlocked, iron chain door.

An inhospitable guardian of the Buddha.

shape of lotus petals and studded with sparkling gems. Necklaces of chunked turquoise, rough rubies, great pearls and bright corals decorate the chest. The face is perfectly symmetrical with elongated, blue-lidded eyes that seemed to cast a spell on all who gazed into them.

After taking photos of the Sakyamuni Buddha with the Lamas, we ceremoniously completed the circle, clockwise around the central hall, and then ascended the stairway to more shrines and crowded chapels. One of these contained the ancient effigies of King Songtsen Gampo, with his Chinese and Nepalese wives, which were said to have been made in the seventh century but looked contemporary. All were arrayed in dazzling silks. The

PHOTO RIGHT:
The Sakyamuni Buddha — in Tibetan, Jawa Rinpoche — said to have been brought to Tibet by Chinese Princess Wen Cheng in the seventh century A.D. when she came to marry King Songtsen Gampo.

156

yuan (approximately $385,000) for major repairs, after extensive damage had been caused from neglect and, during the Cultural Revolution, by "Red Guards." Over the centuries the temple had sunk and the pillars had to be raised to their original position. Drainage pipes were installed to lead the rain water off the roof into the street instead of into the temple.

The inner and outer walls of the central hall and the upper hallways are covered with murals of great historical interest and value depicting Buddhist legends and Tibetan life, the bliss of Nirvana and, in the darker corners, the horrors of hell.

When Tibet was ruled by the lamas, the fear of hell, fire and damnation was injected at an early age into the Tibetan psyche. The people lived in terror of the "Yidaz" or evil spirits, depicted in the temples by images of monsters with big stomachs and heads of animals wearing necklaces of human skulls. The "Yidaz" were believed to infest both the earth and the eighteen hells that awaited sinners. All bad deeds, which included disrespect of the monkhood and refusal to pay taxes, were punished publicly here on earth by whipping and maiming and also below in the eighteen hells. These hells included eight hot ones, where people were tortured by boiling and fire and eight cold ones, where they were frozen by various ingenious methods. Suicide offered no escape, for that led to the worst hell of all — one where people were torn apart, rejoined and then torn apart again — forever and ever.

Effigy of King Songtsen Gampo.

The King's Nepalese wife (Belya).

158

There was a special hell for naughty children. Tales of these hells were digested with the mother's milk, and they existed as real in the minds of the superstitious Tibetans as surely as did the trees and mountains around them. This is why the people felt so blessed to have the Dalai Lama, Living Buddha, who, out of compassion, delayed his entry into Nirvana to help poor sinners like themselves resist earthly desire and material temptation.

The Department of Cultural Relics in Lhasa decided against restoring some of the more erotic tantric murals and the most sadistic scenes of hell, but some can still be seen beneath the sooty walls in a few dark corners. Among the condemned frescoes are those depicting the Bön rites of Chod. Here the Shaman priest, dressed as a devil and wielding a ritual knife (Phurbu), enacts a symbolic dance in a place believed to be haunted by demons, such as a cemetery where corpses are cut up. The forbidden rites, believed by the practitioners to exorcize the evil spirits, involved blood sacrifice, disembowling and the scattering of blood in the air. The fading tantric murals show hideous, many-headed monsters and beasts having sexual intercourse with woman half their size.

The Department also moved the image of Palden Lhamo, the magnificently wicked she-devil, from her prominent private shrine upstairs to an inconspicuous place behind a yak-wool awning in the courtyard. The statue shows her as a wild fury, a hideous black monster clad in the skins of dead men, riding a mule and eat-

Princess Wen Cheng, The King's Chinese wife (Gyalya).

The she-devil Palden Lhamo is often represented as a monster eating brains from a human skull.

Yadiz or evil spirit depicted as a monster.

ing brains from a human skull. She is draped in necklaces of skulls and a jeweled gown. No wonder her dreaded name was so seldom spoken, and then, only in whispers.

The English historian, L.A. Waddell, visited the Jokhang in 1904 and, like Theos Bernard, the American Buddhist, found it dirty and vermin ridden. Waddell wrote that in the shrine of the Great Queen (the she-devil Lhamo):

"... tame mice ran unmolested over the floor, feeding on the cake and grain offerings, under the altar and amongst the dress of the image and up and down the bodies of the monks who were chanting their litany, and were said to be transmigrated nuns and monks ... On the way down we had to run the gauntlet of a whole galaxy of ugly gods, and realized as never before what a debased, thorough-paced idolatry Lamaism has become."

Apparently things had not improved when Bernard visited the temple in 1939. He found the main hall:

"... filthy and hidden in a thick gloom ... The thing that first caught my attention among the upper shrines was the smell of mice, and when my eyes accommodated themselves to the gloom, I could see thousands of these rodents darting in and out among and over the images. Several monks were beating their drums and carrying on the never ending ritual, while they sat among this teaming swarm of mice. And so we left this dungeon of worship and refreshed our souls with a breath of air in the eternal sunlight.

Now the mice have scattered and the chapels have been cleaned up. The walls and pillars shine with fresh paint, and the

The chief monk on the roof of the Jokhang Temple.

monks are constantly picking up the food offerings dropped by worshipers. The whole temple glows like an exquisite jewel.

After a tour of the gaily decorated roof, where the golden symbols of Buddha framed a spectacular view of the Potala Palace, we were taken to the reception room for tea. The chief Lama and Gyatso sat on a dragon-carpeted couch before a bright saffron wall. Over the heads of the crimson-robed monks hung the starkly realistic portraits of China's Chairmen Mao Zedong and Hua Guofeng, looking rather incongruous in this spiritual setting. The lamas talked earnestly about the temple. We learned that in March 1979 the Jokhang was opened for worship after being closed in 1959. Now nine monks manage the temple and welcome the worshipers.

"On the three mornings a week that the temple is open, about 1,000 believers come to pray. On religious holidays there are over 1,400. They are mostly middle-aged and older, but lately some young ones have come." Gyatso said. He spent his spare time "in meditation and reciting the sutras, but I also read the papers and know what is going on in my country." He added that monks were not required to spend time in political study.

Outside, a group of people had waited to see us come out of the temple. Also, some believers were still prostrating themselves on the street in front of the temple, and others were fingering the 108 prayer beads, one for each sutra, and reciting the eternal "Hail to the jewel in the lotus" (om mani padmi hum). Their faces were open, friendly and innocent. They seemed to be waiting for a miracle.

Three lamas sit on the Jokhang Temple roof before their favorite view of the Potala.

Pilgrims prostrate themselves in worship before the temple.

A group of believers wait outside the temple.

PHOTO LEFT: The head lamas sit beneath portraits of Chinese Chairmen Mao Zedong and Hua Guofeng.

8. The Summer Palace

Author with a Chinese guide outside the Summer Palace of the Fourteenth Dalai Lama.

In the past the streets of Lhasa were the scenes of great pageantry, especially during the New Year Festival, when the main event was "Monlam" or the Great Prayer. Then the entire city was placed under control of the monks from the Drepung Monastery, who carried heavy staves and acted as police to control the crowds assembling to witness the celebrations.

During the festivities citizens of all ranks gathered to enjoy the spectacles which went on for weeks, and culminated in a grand fire dance, which commemorated the passing of the old year.

One of Tibet's greatest pageants was when the Dalai Lama made his annual

PHOTO LEFT: The guardian lion was a present from Chiang Kai-shek.

spring journey from his winter palace in the Potala through Lhasa, to his summer palace in Norbulingka, the pleasure garden of the "God-Kings," which was two miles west of the Potala. He would journey in a gilded palanquin that was elaborately carved and curtained, and was preceded by sixteen grand lamas and nobles in their high hats and splendid ceremonial garments.

The Norbulingka, meaning Jewel Park, is a hundred-acre park, thickly shaded by lush trees and aglow with flowers. Marble moon bridges span the clear brooks that flow languidly past graceful pavilions and picnic grounds where the two hundred noble families used to gather on special festivals. Construction of the park was begun in 1755, but each successive ruler

169

added his own buildings. The Fourteenth Dalai Lama, Tenzin Gyatso, built a summer palace from 1954 to 1956, called the Chensil Phodrang, on the site of an old palace. It stands in the middle of the central enclosure containing his personal gardens and surrounded by a high, white brick wall. The main gateway, built by the Thirteenth Dalai Lama, is guarded by two large and comical white lions with pink and blue trimmings that looked more like cartoons created by Walt Disney than, as we were told, personal gifts from Chiang Kai-shek.

PHOTO RIGHT: Front door of the Norbulingka.

The palace itself is a two-story, relatively modest building. The traditional Tibetan architecture has been spiced with rococo ornamentation, Buddhist temple symbols and brightly painted Chinese eaves and pillars. The interior was an incongruous mixture of eastern splendor, religious artifacts and western kitsch. Plastic flowers rise from porcelain vases and ponderous leather furniture, carried across the Himalayas on the backs of porters, line the sacred, frescoed walls.

A regular bed in another room behind the official bed.

An old phonograph inherited from the Thirteenth Dalai Lama stands in bedroom.

PHOTO LEFT: The unmade bed of the Dalai Lama was left as it was when he fled to India on March 17, 1959. The bed is short because Living Buddhas slept with legs crossed in the lotus position.

Painting of the Fourteenth Dalai Lama at age fourteen.

We were informed that everything had been deliberately left as it was on the morning of March 17, 1959, when the Dalai Lama either fled or was taken to India. On his bed the gold brocaded quilt remains rumpled as if it had been hastily flung back. The bed was noticeably short for a grown man, and when I remarked on this, our guide told us that Living Buddhas were required to sleep cross legged in the lotus position. However, he added, that even Living Buddhas were human and showed us a regular long bed in a small room behind the official bed. We had also seen these two types of beds in the bedrooms of the Potala.

Other signs that the Dalai Lama was indeed human were the old fashioned phonograph inherited from his predecessor, which stood beside a fan near the bed. All had been left as it was that fateful dawn when the god-king woke up to the sound of mortar shells plopping into a pond outside the north gate. It has never been established for certain whether the shells were fired by Tibetan rebels who were holding a roadblock north of Norbulingka or the Chinese PLA. The Chinese claim they did not fire until three days later, on March 20th, when the fighting began in

PHOTO RIGHT: Door to the private apartments.

174

Lhasa. Nevertheless the Dalai Lama, not knowing who was firing and fearing for his life, fled with his family to India, leaving his bed unmade. It was learned later that the Dalai Lama's entourage, which included his family and four of his six ministers, had been under Chinese surveillance throughout his fifteen-day journey, and his exact time of arrival at the Indian border was broadcast by Radio Peking. Knowing the spiritual power the Dalai Lama held in Tibet at that time, the Chinese, in particular Premier Zhou En-lai, wisely decided, with an eye to the future, not to do anything that might endanger the life of the twenty-five-year-old God-King. The Dalai Lama was later followed into exile by thousands of nobles and high lamas.

Norbulingka is now open to all the Tibetan people. It is probable that the religious processions with all their pomp and ceremony, are missed by the people who found such colorful occasions broke the boredom of everyday life. On holidays they spread their rugs under the trees in Jewel Park and relax. On such occasions both the men and women enthusiastically partake of a potent local brew called chang. It is made of fermented chingko barley and inevitably inspires rowdy singing and impromptu dances.

For those that prefer more refined entertainment, there are theaters in Lhasa with movies and live concerts. After our visit to the Norbuilingka, we attended a "soiree" of local folk dances. Tibetan and Han performers, dressed in the picturesque costumes of the various national minorities in Tibet, put on spirited folk dances and sang traditional songs to an enthusiastic audience until after midnight.

Murals line the walls of the palace. This one symbolizes longevity.

Tibetan dancers perform local folk dances in a Lhasa theater.

9. Afterthoughts

The night before we left we gazed for the last time at the Potala, casting its moonlit shadow over Lhasa. There it stood, the "High Heavenly Realm", empty and aloof, but still holding its mysterious spell — a proud, haunting beauty — the embodiment of old Tibet. The stars hung like burning sparks in the purple sky, and the rarefied air seemed to crackle with icy shivers. We pulled our sweaters around us and reflected on the past.

The Lama Theocracy that had made its headquarters in the Potala had long been aware that new ideas and outside knowledge were its deadliest enemies. Thought gives rise to doubt and doubt seeks new awareness, which eventually stimulates action. Therefore, the State steadfastly kept its monastic fingers plugged into the dike of ignorance. It was the village

schools set up by the Communists in the 1950's that enabled new knowledge to trickle in and gradually expose the vulnerable and obsolete Theocracy. Within a decade the fossilized foundations of the old society began to crumble. The worst threats to the ruling lamas were realized when the wave of new ideas reached the masses of common people, and they discovered that they, too, could enjoy life; that life could be lived for the present as well as for future incarnations. The country had been ripe for the democratic reforms brought in by the Chinese in the 1960's, but the struggle to obtain them was still long and grueling.

It was, of course, the monasteries that suffered the most during the social transformation that followed the Communist takeover of Tibet. Church and State were forcefully separated. The monasteries were one of the three big owners of serfs and land. They owned 37 per cent of the pastures and cultivated land of Tibet, while 25 per cent was owned by nobility. The remaining 38 per cent was owned by the government, which was run by 333 lamas and 280 lay noblemen. When the land was regrouped into communes run by former serfs, the monasteries lost their source of wealth.

During the Cultural Revolution an open religious persecution, led by China's radicals, took place. An enormous amount of damage was done by the rampaging Red Guards who, against the direct orders of Premier Zhou En-lai, sacked many ancient monasteries and temples including the Jokhang. Learned scholars of Buddhism and leading lamas were persecuted.

After the downfall of the radicals the Communist Party admitted violating its own stated policy of respecting religious beliefs and the cultural heritage in Tibet. It is now attempting to rectify former hostile attitudes towards religion. A new policy of moderation began in 1977, which included an effort to gain popular support of the determined push throughout China for social stability and modernization.

By April of 1979 a total of about $500,000 had been spent restoring the sacred sites of Lhasa, and large sums were allocated for their yearly upkeep. Past unlawful actions against religious policy were repudiated by the Fifth National People's Congress in 1978, and the constitution was restated to guarantee freedom of religious beliefs. A provision of the criminal law now states: "Government personnel who unlawfully infringe on the freedom of belief in religion and the habits of minority nationals . . . shall be sentenced to imprisonment or detention for not more than two years."

Now, according to Article 46 of the Chinese constitution, "citizens enjoy the freedom to believe in religion and the freedom not to believe in religion . . ." The latter was a hitherto unknown freedom in Tibet.

Although religious freedom in Tibet was rudely violated and Buddhism was forced underground for a decade (1966 to 1977), it was far from wiped out. Lamaism, or the rule of the monks, on the other hand, has disappeared with the advance of education. No longer could the monasteries retain power through fear or wealth through exploitation of the unquestioning believers.

Buddhist visitors to Tibet, in the past, have been both enchanted by the hospitality of the ruling class and frustrated by the cruel social contrasts that were calmly accepted as divine judgment.

"There is nothing that fires the heart to such a temperature as does the religious racket (in Tibet)" wrote Buddhist monk Theos Bernard. *". . . It is the deepest rooted evil of mankind — the sooner it is done away with, the more quickly will humanity rise. When I say Religion I mean this organized control, this dictating of sainthood. There is that latent religious feeling in the heart of every man, but there is scarcely a thing to be found in any organized religious system today which we would not do better without. So it might be better for a while to turn our course in the opposite direction and call it by another name so that there will not be any reversion to this faithful path of ignorance."*

Earlier we had asked Shengqing, the Living Buddha, if he thought religion still had a role in Tibetan life.

"To believe or not," he answered, "can only be decided by each individual. As a government we cannot force men to be Buddhist monks. In the future the monks will depend on their own thoughts. In the past many were monks not out of religion but for survival. I am a practising Buddhist myself, but I do not think that organized religion will do any good for our country."

The Peking Government is obviously aware of the lingering influence that Living Buddhas still have over the Tibetan people even if they have changed their message from abstract spiritualism to

184

pragmatic materialism. Shengquing Loshangrancun put it most succinctly when he said, "I no longer believe that I am a Living Buddha, but other people do."

Tibetan Buddhism can no longer be called Lamaism, which has become a derogatory term. Ironically, the forced reformation of Church and State has not only raised living standards but has cleansed the religion of the corrupting influence of Lamaism, as well as the demonic influences of the old Bön religion and the degenerating elements of Tantra. Tibetan Buddhism is, at last, free to return to the Middle Way of Mahayana Buddhism based on the pure, original teachings of Sidhartha Gautama Buddha and the "Four Noble Truths:" suffering, the cause of suffering, the cessation of suffering and the 'Eight Fold Path,' " which leads to the end of suffering. The "Noble Eight Fold Path" consists of right conduct, right speech, right views, right aspirations, right effort, right livelihood, right mindfulness and right rapture.

I left Lhasa feeling that Tibet was on the brink of a new and hopeful era — an enlightened period that will not only bring a rise in living standards and new opportunities for the young people, but also foster a rejuvenation of Tibetan Buddhism and Tibet's unique traditional culture.

Index

X

Y

Z